# Spiritual Psychology

## A Primer

*Meredith J. Sprunger*

Published by Purpose Research, LLC
P. O. Box 19051
Birmingham, Alabama 35219–9051
205/222-8897 http://purposeresearch.com

Cover photo & design © 2009 Charles McLafferty, Jr.

Soft cover edition
ISBN 978–0–9824278–8–0

First printing
Printed in the United States of America

# Spiritual Psychology

## A Primer

*Meredith J. Sprunger*

Purpose Research
Birmingham

## CONTENTS

# INTRODUCTORY OVERVIEW

Spiritual psychology is the study and practice of mental processes relating to Ultimate Reality and eternal values—truth, beauty, and goodness. It is concerned with the search for truth, the achievement of beauty, and the relationships of love. Spiritual growth is the key determiner of personality development and human destiny. Cultivating this aspect of our lives should, therefore, be the chief objective of our educational and developmental aspirations.

## 1. Determinants of Human Behavior

Spiritual enlightenment, however, does not take place in isolation. Everything in human experience exists in intraactive and interactive relationships. In discussing spiritual psychology we should, therefore, be aware of the multiple and complex determinants of human behavior. Heredity establishes the basic limits of individual development. The mechanical integration of skeleton and muscles, the chemical-hormonal regulation of the blood system, and the electrochemical control of the neural system shape our physiological potentials. Physical conditions such as nourishment, exercise, rest, and general health exert an important influence on our lives.

The conditioning factors of environmental-cultural influences are ever-present shapers of human behavior. Our family, friends, and community, along with our unique personal experiences, temper and color much of our lifestyle and most of our decisions. These first-hand cultural experiences, along with the self-determinative factors of the human mind, fashion our behavior. The unique insights of our intellect and the nature of our emotional experiences marshal resources of will that order the direction of our growth.

Everything in the human condition exists in the developmental mode. All of our capacities and potentialities are in the process of becoming or deteriorating. We are dynamic, not static, organisms. In our maturation we pass through characteristic physical, mental, social, and spiritual stages. To work effectively all of the differential aspects of our personality must, to a greater or lesser degree, be integrated and unified. The various attributes of human nature operate in intrarelational and interrelational configurations which function most adequately in a hierarchical order of dominance. Some things and values are more important than others.

The science of psychology strives to evaluate the relative significance of the differential factors in human behavior. Analytical and reductionist approaches to human nature may be useful in research but are inadequate for understanding people in their total environment. Human beings are best understood when viewed holistically. The following diagram may help visualize total personality interaction and development:

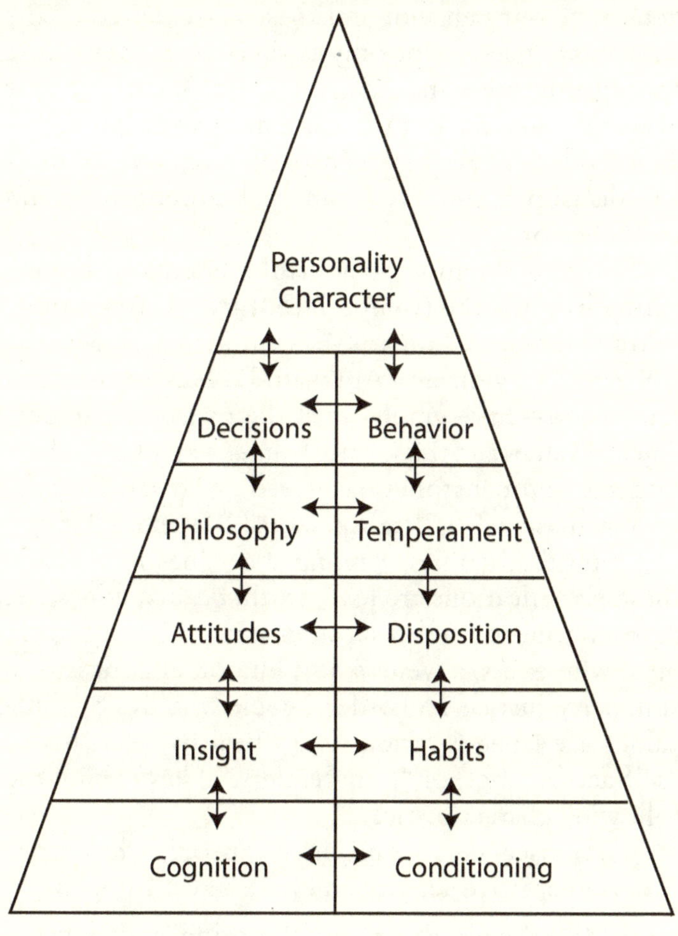

Each person is a complex combination of internal, hereditarial inclinations and external, environmental influences. Our mental capacities alter our conditioning experiences and these cognitive abilities shape our reactions to environmental stimuli. Decisions determine our behavior and these activities color the choices we make. Not only is there total interaction among inherited and environmental factors in our personal make up, but there is a hierarchical or dominance relationship between basic cognitive abilities and decisions, and environmental conditioning and our behavior.

Some of the most insightful students of human nature living in the twentieth century—Carl G. Jung, Viktor Frankl, O. Hobart Mowrer, Henry A. Murray, Roberto Assagioli, and Abraham H. Maslow, to name only a few—have emphasized the overriding importance of values and the spiritual dimension of life. These integrative touchstones have been given various category names such as "transpersonal," "meta," "being," and "spiritual" values. Among the values included in these classifications are love, truth, beauty, goodness, faith, confidence, self-respect, integrity, honesty, openness, wholeness, aliveness, joy, humor, effortlessness, simplicity, justice, and order. People who live by these values are labeled variously as "healthy," "creative," "self-actualizing," or "transcenders." They exhibit the following characteristics:

1. Transcenders are productive people who engage in creative activity and have a zest for living.
2. Transcenders are self-accepting and develop warm and loving interpersonal relationships. They are relatively free from fear and group

coercions but are not authoritarian personalities.

3. Transcenders are intuitive and open to experience. They are attracted to mystery and the unknown. They are innovators and regard themselves as instruments in the actualization of transpersonal values.
4. Transcenders are more interested in meanings than mechanics. They are flexible and open to alternative options. These people view things holistically; they unify, synthesize, and integrate. Self-actualizers work toward goals and purposes.
5. Transcenders are governed by an internal set of values. They are dedicated and live for purposes outside of and larger than themselves. These people are service oriented.
6. Transcenders tend to fuse work and play and experience fulfillment and joy in living. Self-actualizers are less attracted by the rewards of money and things and more motivated by the satisfaction of actualizing Being values.
7. Transcenders have more peak or spiritual experiences and are more oriented toward spiritual reality. They strive for oneness with Being values and Reality which brings the greatest sense of well-being and happiness life can provide.

Metaneeds are rooted in human biology and psychology. They are universal and not the product of the social environment; however, their expression is influenced by culture. Metavalues are the ground of human personality. These values are intrinsic, supracultural, transpersonal, universal, and related to Ultimate Reality. When these values are not actualized in our lives we become frustrated, maladjusted, and ill. The social pathology, existential vacuum, and meaninglessness experienced by contemporary society is the result of intrinsic value starvation, Being-value deficiency. Transpersonal values command adoration, celebration, and reverence. They are worth living and dying for. Contemplating and becoming one with these values gives the greatest sense of worth and joy that human beings can experience. Spiritual psychology, therefore, ought to be the primal study of humanity.

✳ ✳ ✳

## 2. Basic Fields of Knowledge

Underneath the complex and multitudinous variety of human experiences there are four basic fields of knowledge and creativity: science, philosophy, religion, and art.

- Science is the field of description, quantitation, and verification. It establishes our objective world: *this is*.
- Philosophy is the sphere of evaluation. It constructs our world of subjective orientation: *this means*.
- Religion is the realm of value perception, commitment, and dedication. It determines our personal values and way of living: *this way*.
- Art is the province of form and expression. It creates the atmosphere and method of communication and execution: *this is; this means; this way*.

These basic ways of perceiving and thinking interact in their working methodologies. The scientific method proceeds through observation, hypothesis, experiment, evaluation, and verification. Its objective is to predict and control.

The philosophic method starts with the latest scientific facts, applies rational and creative thought and arrives at an evaluation, theory, or truth. Its objective is to understand, formulate goals, and unify human experience.

The religious method starts with the most reliable science (without this foundation you end up with mythology, superstition, or a degenerate, outmoded religion), and applies the most rational and coherent philosophy. Without this refining process you may evolve an irrational religion or an uncontrolled mysticism. It then artfully organizes personal experience with these established facts and highest values of philosophy and revelation (personal and/or epochal) and makes a total dedication to this way of life. Its objective is to become like, and find union with, Reality.

The artistic method starts with selected scientific facts and a particular philosophic-religious point of view and creates the most attractive and effective forms of expression which embody these facts and meanings for a specific life purpose. Its objective is to enhance and expedite the purpose of the artistic production.

These basic sources of human knowledge stem from the nature of human perception. We experience the material world, mind consciousness, and spiritual reality—truth, beauty, and goodness. Our lives are shaped by relationships with things, meanings, and values. Characteristically, we proceed from the observation and assimilation of facts to truth insight, and after verifying the reliability of these truths in living, we arrive at the wisdom of experience. This wisdom teaches us that the material world is eventually subject to mind mastery and that mind is ultimately controlled by spiritual reality. The universe, we learn, is not like the mechanistic-scientific model but more akin to the personality model of creative, syncretistic thought and action.

Religion is the highest, most healing and integrating activity of humankind. The core of religion is personal, spiritual experience; spiritual psychology (personal experience with values and Reality) is the essence of religion. It has sociological and institutional repercussions but should not be confused with these second-order group manifestations. Religion or spiritual psychology should be distinguished from science, philosophy, art, social service, economics, and politics. It is superior to, but not independent of, all of them. Where science and philosophy leave off, religion begins. While art engages in the manipulation and enhancement of material things, religion is involved in the enrichment and transformation of the experiential world.

The world today is in dire need of new religious leaders who perceive the essential truths of spiritual psychology and the eternal reality to which they point: the Universal Father of all. Contemporary society is looking for a religion which is harmonious with the facts of science, consistent with the highest truths of philosophy, and permeated with the atmosphere of unconditional love. The true prophets of our day do not engage in the celebration of the irrational, simplistic, authoritarian answers of the Middle Ages. They recognize the limitations of intelligence and rational thought and press on to catch the transforming vision of a new and expanded conceptualization of reality. A spiritually mature religion has the following characteristics:

1. A mature religion excludes the element of magic and superstition and is solidly rooted in history and experience.
2. A mature religion has a universal, inclusive point of view.
3. A mature religion does not confuse symbols with reality.

4. A mature religion achieves unity without demanding uniformity.
5. A mature religion has an ethic of love.
6. A mature religion is committed to the principles of physical, psychological, and spiritual health. It integrates and builds the individual, producing peace of mind and joy in living.
7. A mature religion stimulates individual freedom, creative expression, and growth.

Western civilization is largely secular. Even our religious institutions are deeply involved in secular, nonspiritual activities such as social welfare, economics, and politics. The creative renewal of our social institutions will take place only when individuals are transformed by an enhanced vision of spiritual reality. Inspired by augmented spiritual resources, the leaders of society will reform and redirect our social institutions. Religious leaders engaged in counseling all too often employ only secular psychological methodologies and insights. They, thereby, largely bypass the great spiritual therapeutic resources available to humankind. Scientific psychological discoveries should certainly be utilized but they are only an adjunct to spiritual psychological reality insights and relationships.

This treatise is intended to remind those of us who are unconsciously secular in our psychological orientation that living up to our real human potentials can only take place when we have a first-hand, personal relationship with the source of all reality—the Universal Father. The principles of spiritual psychology presented in this small book attempt to outline the dynamics of spiritual living.

❋ ❋ ❋

## A.
## THE SEVEN BASIC REALITIES
## (The Given)

### 1. Reality Essence:
### The Universal Father and the Paradise Trinity

Human consciousness is oriented by the reality frame of reference within which it lives. We think and act according to the fact and value parameters of our perceptual and conceptual world. Psychology always functions within a metaphysical context. Our conscious and unconscious comprehension of Ultimate Reality conditions all of our thought and action. This ontological or intuitive frame of reference is a faith conviction. It is the universal philosophical ground of the human mind.

The theological or religious term which our culture uses to symbolize this First Source and Center of all things and beings is "God." Principles of spiritual psychology are determined by the nature of God and the nature and quality of our minds. Each person has slightly or markedly different faith convictions concerning the nature of God and different mind experiences and qualities. The author's sharing of faith convictions regarding the nature of God and universe dynamics is not intended to persuade the reader to accept them but as a means of communicating, and possibly explaining, truths which are empirically operative in spiritual psychology and common in human experience.

Our minds are, obviously, finite, limited, and subject to error. No human language is adequate to express the realities of infinity. There are no incontrovertible scientific or logical proofs of God and spiritual realities; however, there is much scientific and logical data which make such faith convictions reasonable and highly probable. In spite of these limitations, every human being can experience the presence of God and the enrichment of spiritual values.

The human mind has the innate ability to formulate a universe frame in which to think. Every electron, planet, thought, personality, and spirit reality is a functioning unit in this holistic universe; no entity or being exists or lives in isolation. Grasping the infinity of the universe is beyond the capacity of finite minds. The limitlessness of Deity and Reality stagger the human imagination. There are, no doubt, Deity Absolutes which we cannot fathom. The Hindu concept of Brahman strives to probe such a reservoir of potentiality. Our astronomical universe seems to extend into infinity. These galaxies of outer space probably contain many inhabited planets. Our assumption is that we live in a gigantic creation which is populated by innumerable forms of intelligent life. The spiritual cosmos must parallel and exceed this material creation. Human life is an adventure into the unknown, but we are not alone.

While God consciousness is not our most immediate awareness, God is the most real and certain of all our experiences. In, through, and under our everyday, mundane consciousness, we become aware of an authentic self deep within. We gradually come to recognize this inner identity and presence as our ground of being, the irreducible reality in our consciousness. This is the most important and rewarding human experience—to find God for oneself, in oneself, and of oneself.

God is primal in relation to all psychological functions, relationships, and realities. The kingdom of God is actualized by the rule of God in the human heart. Nothing can take the place of God in individual consciousness or human society. To be separated from God is to be cut off from the source of life and creativity. When such an alienation takes place we have a deteriorating personality and a cut-flower civilization. Conversely, when we acknowledge God's primal relationship in our lives, we receive all other things essential to creative growth and eternal survival along with it.

God's basic and dominant relationship with all personalities is that of love. We, therefore, spontaneously acknowledge the inherent and indigenous universe relationship as the Father/Motherhood of God and the brother/sisterhood of all people, the Parenthood of God and the kinship of all humanity. In this conscious relationship, we progressively grow in our ability to experience the presence of God and enrich our lives through this divine fellowship.

We recognize the totality of spiritual influence in our lives as unitary and holistic; however, humanity over the centuries has experienced and conceptualized a multiple deity relationship, traditionally referred to as the Paradise Trinity: the Universal Father, the Eternal Son, and the Infinite Spirit. This trinitarian recognition is an important distinction in understanding the dynamics of spiritual psychology. It helps us visualize and relate to the spiritual realities in human experience.

The Trinity ministers to the mind of each individual. The Father indwells the human mind with a fragment or spark of his Spirit, which we will refer to as the Indwelling Spirit or Inner Light. The Son enhances our insight with the Spirit of Truth. This Spirit of Truth ministers to our mind through the Holy Spirit, which is closely attuned to the chemical-electrical circuits of the brain-mind. All of this spirit ministry is unified and we experience it as one guiding and sustaining presence.

The Paradise Trinity has further created and structured the universe to be favorable to spirit-related psychological functions. The Father is the source of the personality-gravity circuit, drawing all personalities to himself. The Son is the center of the spirit-gravity circuit, pulling all spirit-attuned psychological activity to his presence. The greater the spirit content of our consciousness, the stronger we are drawn to all truth. In this sense spirit gravity operates very much like material gravity. The Spirit activates the mind-gravity circuit, drawing all thought harmonious with reality toward Ultimate Reality. These universe spiritual-gravity systems are perfectly unified, directing all spiritually-oriented thinking and personality development toward greater and greater spiritual realization.

Another aspect of the infinite complexity of deity which is important in considering the principles of spiritual psychology is the cosmic universe yeast referred to by William James, Carl G. Jung, Alfred N. Whitehead, and others as the developing, evolutionizing, perfecting nature of God. This activity of divine leavening, the Supreme, stimulates personal, planetary, and universe growth toward perfection. The Supreme is the divine energizing influence undergirding action, competence, and achievement. The deity presence of the Supreme coordinates the divine and changeless realities of eternity with the finite and ever-changing events of time.

### *Summary Statement*

Spiritual psychology is conditioned, first of all, by the nature of reality. God as the First Source and Center of all things and beings is the primal relationship and ultimate determiner of all that is human. The Universal Father, being of spirit nature, assures that all human thought and action culminates in some form of spiritual growth and achievement. Spiritual psychology seeks to understand the dynamics of this foundational fact of the human condition.

✳ ✳ ✳

## 2. Reality Forms: Matter, Mind, And Spirit

We experience three basic forms of reality: matter, mind, and spirit, which take the psychological expressions of fact, meaning, and value. All are aspects of energy having a common origin in the creative activity of God, but are quite different in their contributions to our spiritual-psychological growth and destiny. Matter, mind, and spirit are dynamically intrarelated in human experience; however, no one of these aspects of reality can be reduced to any other. To observe that mind emerged from matter may appear to be a fact of science but it is not the truth of its nature or origin. All mind has a nonmaterial creative source even though it is associated with matter and is, to a significant degree, materially conditioned. Likewise, although spirit values find expression through mind activity, their origin is in the spirit category of reality.

Human nature is dominated quantitatively by material experience. We are material beings. We live in material bodies and think by means of electrochemical activity of the material brain-mind. While the activity of matter is highly mechanical and can be predicted by physical laws, its behavior is dynamic at the atomic and subatomic level. Although the material world is stable and tangible to ordinary perception, at the atomic level it is energy in motion and its behavior cannot always be predicted by analytical logic. Reason is unable to predict the substance created or the behavioral characteristics of many compounds formed by the union of various chemical elements. There is no analytical way of knowing that two atoms of flammable hydrogen combined with one atom of oxygen, which supports combustion, would form a liquid, water, which will extinguish fire! Neither is there anything about its chemical composition which would suggest, unlike most substances which shrink when cooled, that water would expand when frozen. So the entire realm of nature warns against the folly of postulating a mechanistic universe and eloquently implies that behind all is a great mind.

Mind is a form of reality which, substantially, we still know little about. It has origin in the cosmic mind of the Infinite Spirit. Experientially and functionally, however, we have a greater first-hand knowledge of mind than we do of matter and spirit. We live in the arena of mind, the cognitive activity of psychological consciousness, perception, and thought. Everything we know about matter and spirit is mediated to us by our mind. It is through mental techniques that material reality and spirit reality become experiential. Mind bridges the broad gap in the finite world between material and spiritual reality. It unifies fact and value through meaning. Cognitive philosophy integrates our total experience.

Mind has many and complex relationships with matter and spirit. We have experiential and empirical evidence that physical changes result in mental alterations and that mental attitudes effect physiological changes. States of mind condition our perception of spiritual values and spiritual transformation significantly alters our mental orientation.

As our mind relates holistically with matter and spirit, two basic cognitive capacities emerge: intelligence and creativity. Intelligence is more closely associated with fact perception and left-brain activity and generates logic and analytical, rational thought. Creativity is more intimately related to value perception and right-brain activity and originates insight and integral, synergistic thinking. When the development of intelligence proceeds faster than spiritual growth, the individual has difficulty perceiving the depth of truth, beauty, and goodness in human experience and often becomes cynical of religious idealism. Likewise, overspiritual development tends to produce a fanatical person who is out of harmony with facts and who distorts spiritual insight.

The universe, when examined from the objective reasoning methodology of fact perception, yields the point of view of the physical sciences which can be largely standardized for all people. When reality is studied from the "inside" view of psychological consciousness and value perception, we have the varied world views of psychology, philosophy, and theology. These separate views of different minds and a wide variety of experiences greatly augment the creativity of civilization and culture. These divergent points of view become counterproductive and dangerous only when based on selective extremes in perceptual thinking resulting in philosophical materialism, psychism, or spiritism, which always distort reality.

It is in the personality, where the physical, mental, and spiritual realities are in triune harmony of development, that the maximum of wisdom, achievement, and effectiveness can be realized. The highest philosophical achievement of humanity must be based on the facts of science, the coherence of rational thought, the faith of religion, and the truth insight of revelation. Mind is the human capacity which never ceases to grow. It is the experiential technique of endless progress.

Spirit is the qualitative form of reality representative of the nature of God. It is the highest expression of divine creativity. Spirit is the architect of human destiny, giving meaning and purpose to life. It is the source of self-fulfillment, inner peace, and happiness. On the finite level, matter is dominant except in personality, where spirit, through the mediation of mind, is striving for control. Unless we use value perception to discriminate ends of behavior, we tend to function at the animal level of existence. Spiritual realization makes it possible for us to transcend our animal origins. As our minds become more aligned with Spirit, they are less responsive to the material gravity of physiological drives and we experience greater freedom from the material mechanisms of brute behavior.

In the intradynamics of matter, mind, and spirit in human experience, matter is eventually controlled by mind and mind is ultimately mastered by the overcontrol of spirit. Our lives are endowed with spiritual-psychological resources whereby we can, if we are willing and persistent, gradually evolve our crass material-animal inheritance into noble, spirit-directed natures. The divine plan for our lives is to lead us in the ages ahead to the achievement of spirit-personality status.

### *Summary Statement*

A balanced spiritual psychology must take into consideration information from physical, mental, and spiritual aspects of reality. It clearly and realistically accepts and understands the material nature of humankind even while realizing that the well-being and fulfillment of human nature rests on the insights and guidance of spiritual reality. This paradoxical dichotomy is transcended through the mediation of the psychological dynamics of mind.

* * *

### 3. Reality Methodology: Evolution

The most fundamental truth of the universe is that there is a divine plan operative everywhere and God's will and way shall eventually prevail. The entire cosmos is designed to function as a living organism. This purposive design has been, is now, and will always be in creative process. In the finite universe the divine plan is undergirded by two foundational realities: the deity presence of the Supreme, who acts as the catalyzer of all development and progress; and evolution, which is ordained as the divine methodology of all finite growth and change.

The ground of universe evolution is intelligent purpose and its underlying objective is progress. The basic demand of life is growth, development, and maturation. God's directive to all mortals is that we grow toward perfection. Curiosity, the urge to explore, and the drive for ever-increasing environmental adjustment and adaptation, is innate in evolutionary creatures and evidences the existence within them of an inherent striving for growth and perfection. The story of humankind's ascent from one-celled organisms in the sea to the rational and creative domination of the earth is a thrilling and inspiring odyssey, witnessing to the wisdom and grandeur of the Universal Father's plan for his sons and daughters of earth. Living experience is designed for educational purposes and the entire universe serves as one vast school for evolving mortals.

Evolution is the key modus operandi of the finite universe. It is the divine creative process for achieving growth. That is why perception, learning, growth, development, and maturation are so fundamental in human life. There is no substitute for experience. As we participate in evolutionary growth, we become partners with God in our own creative process of becoming. We learn that everything starts with the small and insignificant, the quiet and undramatic. From these mustard-seed beginnings most of our accomplishments are made with inadequate resources, means, associates, and abilities.

Our animal nature seeks ease, pleasure, and the line of least resistance. Change is always more or less disturbing and traumatic. Pain and suffering, therefore, invariably accompany, and often stimulate, spiritual growth and evolutionary progress. The catalytic power of adversity and the spiritual value of disappointment and defeat are among the less recognized and appreciated constructive aspects of evolutionary development. Human beings require much time and repeated experience to make significant changes in their habitual ways of thought and behavior conditioned by custom and tradition. Nevertheless, those who are motivated by living faith discover that it becomes gradually easier to do the right things. Although our actual achievement is slow, the overriding imperative is that we are facing and moving in the direction of God's will and way.

There is a basic law of readiness operative in all growth and development. Maturation and achievement are dependent on the evolutionary reality elements germane to such accomplishment. We learn and grow through involvement, by hands-on, minds-on participation. There is a natural, slow, and sure way of actualizing divine purpose in individual growth and social development. There are no short cuts to the divine methodology of evolution. When we attempt to skip grades in our learning experience, we eventually labor under handicaps or fail. Proceeding too rapidly leads to a breakdown in growth and development. Conversely, when people or institutions achieve development and learning levels, they cannot be arbitrarily held back very long. Violence, revolution, apathy, or other similarly noncreative responses occur when such restraints are imposed.

God has established creative purpose in the laws and evolutionary dynamics of the universe. There is a movement from the simple to the complex—from the atom to the galaxy, from the amoeba to man. Development proceeds from the physical through the mental-psychological to the spiritual. Primitive society and youth emphasize physical activities and pleasure. Civilized society and mature adults stress the discipline and development of intellectual capacities, education, and culture. The sages and saints cultivate the spiritual achievements of actualizing truth, beauty, and goodness, fostering brotherhood, and finding God.

We grow from selfishness and egocentricity toward love and universality, from self-expression to self-mastery, from negative fear motivation to positive self-actualization achievement. Maslow points out that the evolution of human motivation takes the following order of priority: physiological needs, safety needs, love needs, self-esteem needs, self-actualization needs, and spiritual (meta, being, or value) needs. There is a planetary dynamic moving from randomness, lawlessness, and arbitrariness toward order, lawfulness, design, and justice. Primitive or immature people see life determined by whim and caprice and make rules to fit their personal advantage. An advanced or spiritually mature civilization perceives a universe governed by law and purpose and recognizes justice even when it is inimical to its immediate personal welfare.

There is a holistic evolutionary trend from external control to internal control, from group rights to individual rights, from force and coercion to freedom and creativity. Immature people need strict rules and regulations. The culturally advanced person does the good and wise thing of his or her own volition. To the spiritually mature person Augustine said, "Love God and do as you like." These purposeful dynamics of universe evolution, however, seldom function on a simplistic, straight-line basis. There is fluctuation back and forth, sometimes resulting in deep cultural regression, before the supremacy of divine purpose establishes a stable ascendancy. The endless complexity of intrarelated integration and interrelated adjustments takes eons of time before the dominance of the inherent integral, synergistic characteristics of evolutionary reality become manifest.

The evolutionary nature of the finite universe requires constant growth and never-ending adjustments. Every generation needs to learn anew the art of living. Much help and guidance can be received from truth principles taught by our elders and verified in the historical process. But truth is living and cannot be captured in static concepts or dogmas. This divine, eternal, living truth unfolds itself in new manifestations from decade to decade so it can minister to the peculiar needs and conditions of each successive generation. It constantly requires new and fresh interpretations and applications.

### *Summary Statement*

Spiritual psychology is predicated on evolutionary insight and methodology. Growth and transformation are not only possible, but the basic laws of the universe undergird such change. We should not become discouraged by the lack of short-term results. Our attention needs to be directed toward areas that are ready for improvement. The evolutionary process in human development and social change is measured in small increments. Patience, perseverance, courage, and faith are the watchwords of spiritual maturity. The mill wheel of the Supreme grinds exceedingly slow but gloriously fine.

* * *

## 4. Personal Reality Identity: We Are Sons and Daughters of God

What all human beings most need to keep in their consciousness is that they are sons and daughters of God. This is our true and inalienable identity. The two things human beings cannot run away from or escape are themselves, their personal identity consciousness, and God, their indwelling, authentic ground of being. Regardless of our temporary state of weakness, poverty, social rejection, or depravity, we are children of our Heavenly Father and as such we are of supreme worth. Each person is a child of God without duplicate in infinity. The Universal Father's loving bestowal of his Indwelling Spirit to minister to our minds reveals the transcendent value which he places on each of his mortal children.

We find and maintain a superb self-respect as we consciously or unconsciously accept and live in this spiritual identity as a son or daughter of God. This self-respect is also coordinate with the love and service which we give to our fellow human beings. We cannot fully accept ourselves when we fail to love our associates; neither can we unconditionally love our neighbors unless we have high self-esteem. Everything constructive in our lives stems from this authentic psychological-spiritual identity as children of the Universal Father. Nothing in all the universe can separate us from this life-enhancing relationship except our failure to courageously and persistently live in its psychological reality.

When we know who we are, we recognize that we exist in a spiritual, organic, vine-and-branches relationship. As we maintain this living spiritual connection with the First Source and Center of all things and beings, we bear abundant fruit. Those who enter into partnership with God discover great things happening in their earthly sojourn. Our primary concern should be to remain open to the will of the Father in our lives. His Indwelling Spirit has an ideal but optional plan for us to work out. This divine creative pattern can be actualized in various vocations and social activities. The thrilling potentials of our earth careers are closely associated with this divinely inspired plan of development. It is the source of wise self-actualization and the basic condition of self-fulfillment and happiness. When we give God all that we have, then God makes us more than we are.

Human beings straddle two categories of existence. While we are children of God, we are also a part of nature and members of the animal kingdom. We are finite, but we are indwelt by a spark of infinity. Humankind exists in the material world; nevertheless, we can transcend nature. Even philosophical materialism is an eloquent demonstration of the nonmaterial aspect of mind. If mind were a purely material-mechanical machine or mechanism, it would not be self-consciously aware of other dimensions of existence. Human nature has the potential for both good and evil. Finitude is not inherently evil, but it is limited and imperfect. It is the misuse, distortion, and perversion of the finite which gives rise to evil and sin.

It is important to recognize and discriminate among the basic ways in which finite beings become disharmonious with universe law. Evil is the condition of functioning contrary to the will of God through ignorance. It indicates our lack of knowledge and is a measure of our imperfection. Sin is an attitude and action whereby we consciously violate divine guidance and universe regulations. It is an indication of our lack of a serious and dedicated desire to be spiritually directed. Such destructive behavior reflects a disinclination to follow the will of God or our inability to master animal and irrational tendencies. Iniquity is a state of cosmic insanity in which sin is embraced as a dedicated way of life. It is rebellion against God and a rejection of his loving plan for our spiritual growth and salvation.

Before we consciously undergo a spiritual reorganization of our thinking and action, we are sometimes dominated by tendencies toward evil. Potential evil is inherent in the natural order of the finite universe; in its present state the time-space creation is imperfect. Human nature, however, has even greater tendencies toward good, which lead us to an awareness of our spiritual ground of being and undergirds our desire for spiritual transformation. The greatest danger of human nature is pride. Egotism undermines our spiritual integrity and, if not checked, becomes thoroughly corrupting. It confuses and disguises our will for God's will and poisons spiritual insight and growth. There are no substitutes, short cuts, or improvements on the divine way to spiritual growth, salvation, and perfection.

When we live in the full realization that we are sons and daughters of God, we are delivered from the morbid introspection of those who are dominated by a sense of finite depravity, unworthiness, and guilt. In the place of self-examination and self-denial, the God-knowing person strives to substitute self-forgetfulness, self-control, and eventually self-mastery. We should not become discouraged by the fact that we are human. When our lives are transformed by the Spirit, we are strengthened and empowered by the constant spiritual renewing of our minds so that we no longer are slaves to our animal drives, but through self-mastery we experience the new liberty, freedom, and worthfulness of those who are in fact and in truth the children of the Universal Father.

Through this spirit-born, enhanced self-realization we live in the psychological-spiritual security of those who are certain about their eternal welfare. These God-knowing people are not overwhelmed by misfortune and suffering; they do not become depressed by disappointment or defeat. They are challenged and stimulated by problems and frustrations and exhibit tenacious courage and invincible faith in the face of the uncertain and unknown. They know that all things eventually work together for the growth and good of the sons and daughters of God.

The concomitant fact of our spiritual identity as children of God is that we are all members of the Universal Father's family. We recognize that all of the Father's mortal sons and daughters are our brothers and sisters. This planetary fact and spiritual truth requires that we constantly expand our in-group perceptions and realize that we can have social and institutional unity without racial, cultural, intellectual, or religious uniformity. Our welfare is closely related to living in loving relationships with the members of our family, neighborhood, community, and world.

### *Summary Statement*

The foundation of spiritual psychology is the realization that we are children of God; as such, we have supreme worth. We live out of this relationship in all areas of our experience. God's creative purpose for our lives gives meaning to all that we do. Being his sons and daughters delivers us from morbid introspection and guilt because of our limitations and deficiencies. As children of the Universal Father we are inspired and empowered to renewed effort, self-forgetfulness, self-control, and self-mastery.

✻ ✻ ✻

## 5. Personal Eternal Realities: Our Superconscious Spirit, Soul, and Personality

Human beings are material organisms. We are the creation of the long, divinely initiated and controlled evolutionary process. Homo sapiens has achieved rational intelligence and truth-, beauty-, and goodness-value perception. Through these cognitive abilities we have built an enduring civilization and culture. Yet we, as individuals, are temporary inhabitants of planet earth. Our material bodies and minds are passing phenomena. We are laying the foundations for a more permanent existence. The only surviving aspects of our mortal experience are our superconscious Spirit, our semi-spiritual soul, and our divinely bestowed personality, which carry all of our self-identity, value, and interpersonal memories to the next stage of our development.

### The Superconscious Spirit

One of the greatest mysteries of the universe is that a fragment of God lives in the human mind. The Ultimate Reality farthest from us is also the Indwelling Spirit most intimately associated with us. This Father Fragment is the absolute focal point in human destiny. It is the kingdom of God within. The superconscious Spirit is the deepest and most real aspect of the human mind. This indwelling presence is the means by which we can know and fellowship with God. Our Inner Light is the cosmic window through which we can glimpse the realities of eternity. It is the source by which we can receive an eternal perspective while living amid the limitations and handicaps of time.

The Indwelling Spirit is the nucleus of our superconscious mind. All ideas, concepts, values, and relationships which are harmonious with the Indwelling Spirit constitute our superconscious mind. Our superconscious psychological activities have permanence in the universe. The Father's Spirit always respects our will and never tries to control our thinking, but seeks to spiritualize and eternalize it. When our will coincides with the Father's will we receive the reinforcement of the Spirit's support. Because of the presence of the Indwelling Spirit we can live in unbroken communion and fellowship with our Heavenly Father. As we are mindful of his indwelling presence and love, we are never alone.

When we first try to commune with the indwelling presence of God, it is difficult and seldom yields conscious results of success. These sincere attempts to fellowship with the Indwelling Spirit, nevertheless, are effective. We gradually establish a rapport with the Inner Guide who is an efficient minister to the higher phases of the mind. This faithful custodian of values for our future career duplicates every worthy mental creation with its spiritual counterpart. The Father is thus slowly and surely remaking us with those values of Spirit reality which are basic to our resurrection on higher universe levels. The Indwelling Spirit, while interested in our temporal welfare and real achievements on earth, is primarily devoted to our soul growth and eternal progress. This loving Divine Guide is the essence of our eternal personality development.

The partnership between the Indwelling Spirit and the mind and personality is the most amazing fact of human experience. Its eternal potential is simply beyond our mortal understanding and comprehension. This divine-human enterprise makes character transformation possible, and through this transcendence of our animal nature our planetary environment and relationships can also be transformed. We ought, therefore, to do everything possible to cooperate with God's presence in our lives.

How thoughtless it is to contaminate the body, which is the temporary residence of the Spirit of God and the potentially immortal soul, with physical poisons. How irresponsible of us to permit the psychological poisons of anxiety, fear, hatred, bigotry, and a host of other negative attitudes to defile and dominate our minds. These physical and psychological poisons greatly handicap the Spirit's activity in our personality development.

As we progressively avoid the pitfalls of evil and sin and increasingly identify with truth, beauty, and goodness and actualize these values in our lives, we become more unified in our spiritual growth and more in harmony with the will of God. The great goal and all-important objective of our mortal adventure is to achieve union with the Indwelling Spirit of God. When our wills truly, without reservation, become one with the Father's will and our personality growth harmonizes with this unitary reality, we experience fusion with the Spirit Entity which God has bestowed on us. For most of us this will occur on higher universe levels. Fusion with our Father's Spirit marks the end of the probationary period of human destiny. We then have eternal status in the universe and our more advanced spiritual education begins.

## The Soul

The people of all races and cultures have believed there is something substantial in human nature which survives mortal death. This vital aspect of life has been given many names. In Western Civilization we designate this enduring entity as the *soul*. The English word *psychology*, when literally translated from its Greek origins, means "the study of the soul." Scientific psychology, however, with its objective methodology will never discover the existence of the soul. It can be known only through superconscious insight and spiritual awareness. The soul is difficult to demonstrate but it can be personally experienced.

The soul is the self-conscious, truth-discerning, goodness-affirming, and spirit-perceiving aspect of the human mind. It is factualized by a divine-human partnership. The Inner Light reveals truth, beauty, and goodness to the human mind and the human will wholeheartedly affirms these spirit realities in experience. Because of the divine involvement in soul development, it is a semispiritual reality which transcends material existence. The material mind is the soil in which the Indwelling Spirit, with our cooperation, evolves the immortal soul. By analogy, mind is our vehicle of experience; the Indwelling Spirit is our road map and compass; our will is the chauffeur determining the roads we travel and our destination.

The evolutionary growth of the soul is not a conscious process. As the soul develops it functions somewhat like a second mind, partially displacing the subconscious mind inherited from our animal origins. New phases of soul consciousness enable us to experience higher levels of spirit awareness. To facilitate soul growth in human experience we need to subordinate the material and temporal to the spiritual and eternal in our will decisions and living. The spiritual objective of human life is to evolve a selfhood of survival value. As the soul matures there is an increasing transfer of the seat of identity from the perishable physical body and material mind to the semispiritual soul which survives the death of our transient life vehicles.

## Personality

Personality is the gift of the Universal Father. It is absolutely unique in each individual and is the permanent aspect of each person in the midst of constant change. Personal beings can transcend material experience because spirit is the basic personality quality. Personality may be associated with material, mindal, and spiritual realities and exhibits many organizing, integrating, synergizing, and dominant functions. Personality is the pattern characteristic of being, determining the psychophysiological arrangement of energies and behavioral expression. It organizes and integrates our psychophysical systems and unifies our sense of self-identity and self-continuity. This divine gift gives value to identity and imparts meanings to our continuity of experience. The bestowal of personality gives human beings the capacity for self-determination, soul growth, and self-identity with the Indwelling Spirit of the Father.

Personality is not entirely subject to the conditioning of antecedent causation; it is not a mechanistic slave of material cause-and-effect relationships.

Persons can transcend the deterministic sequence of events. There are no inherent limitations to the evolution of personality realities. The dynamic free will of personalities makes it impossible to completely predict their decisions and actions. The uniqueness of personality stimulates originality and creativity in living. The same spiritual truth finds different interpretation and expression in each person.

The purpose of the Supreme in universe evolution is to unify personality through increasing spirit dominance. Personality is the Father's gift which has inherent capabilities to use spiritual resources for the mastery of our physical nature through the mediation of mind. The development of dominance over all psychophysical systems and the unification of all experience is an innate propensity of personality. All that is purely material, unassociated with spirit reality, in human experience is a means to an end. Personality has spiritual relationships and is destined for unification with the Indwelling Spirit; therefore, it has immortal potentials.

Personality develops through experience, particularly in soul growth and spirit attunement. This spiritual maturation results in a superb integration of personality and enhanced effectiveness. We become more real, more authentic, more constructively productive in living. Such character integrity eventuates in increasing personal freedom as it is associated with greater reality perception, self-understanding, and self-mastery. The overall purpose of mortal experience is to develop an integrated, well-balanced personality rooted in spiritual reality.

### *Summary Statement*

The dominant elements in spiritual psychology are the Indwelling Spirit, the evolving soul, and the personality. Amid the vicissitudes of living we need to keep in mind these realities, which are basic and determinative in our destiny. The Indwelling Spirit is our guide and compass. With our cooperation and affirmation of spiritual truth, our soul is factualized. All of our capabilities and potentialities are organized, integrated, and synergized through personality dominance. These permanent aspects of our lives prepare us for the struggles of time and the adventures of eternity.

✳ ✳ ✳

## 6. Personal Temporal Realities: Our Material Body and Material Brain-Mind

The human body and mind are rooted in the electrochemical nature of matter and are the product of organic evolution. We are both the creation of past history and individuals in the process of becoming. Heredity determines many of the tendencies, potentials, and limitations of our body, mind, emotional disposition, and general behavior. The divine creative process uses this evolutionary methodology to set the stage for the potential of personal-volitional soul growth and spiritual development.

Human beings are dynamic organisms. Many psychological-affective reactions and experiences are determined by biochemical conditions. Likewise, mental-emotional attitudes can influence physical conditions, including the autonomic nervous system, which regulates such things as heart rate, blood pressure, and hormonal secretions. The human body-brain is a holistic bioelectrochemical organism which is mind endowed and spirit indwelt.

While our inherited animal drives cannot be eradicated, they can be modified and our mental and emotional responses to such urges can be significantly changed. Although finite morals are far from perfection and should never be associated with infallibility, our natural urges, appetites, and impulses are not inherently in conflict with the highest ethical behavior and spiritual development. Indeed, we have inherited a solid psychological foundation for moral and spiritual growth. Various forms of ethical behavior, such as cooperation and caring activities, and spirit-searching inclinations, such as the lure of the unknown and the urge to worship, have been partially programmed into our genes.

We should not be discouraged because we are finite and human. The fact that we are mortal sons and daughters of God, the lowest intelligent beings with survival potential, should fill us with joy and anticipation; our finitude is the basis for the realization that we have been given a virtually unlimited range of spiritual growth potential. We face an eternity and infinity of adventure in which to discover the destiny which the Universal Father has in store for us.

Heredity may limit the rate of our soul growth and personality unification in our mortal lives but it cannot prevent our salvation and ascendant career. This determination rests with our freewill faith decisions and sincere desires. Just as the water lily has its roots in the dark muck of the lake bottom yet raises its snowy head in the bright sunshine, so humankind, while having its origins in the soil of animal nature, can by faith and psychological orientation live in the sunlight of truth, beauty, and goodness and bear the ennobling fruits of the spirit.

Although human consciousness and mental activity are made possible by the electrochemical processes of the brain and neural system, the crucially significant capacity of the mortal mind is its spirit identity potential. While the material mind is not spiritual in nature, it is the host of a Spark of God and the gateway to the development of the spiritual aspects of the superconscious mind and the soul. The psychological activities of our mind, soul, and Indwelling Spirit are closely interassociated and usually cannot be consciously differentiated. Scientific knowledge of our higher mental functions is still very limited. There are, however, distinguishable subjective stages, psychic progressions, or psychological levels of cosmic awareness associated with spiritual achievement.

Starting with faith and trust, our will decisions directionalize our superconscious growth and personality competence. At a critical point in our spiritual journey we dedicate our lives to God and thereby establish our spiritual identity and purpose. Priorities and values are restructured. Our lives are motivated and directed by truth, beauty, and goodness—God. Our personality achieves spiritual maturity as we are dominated by love and service. The highest level of personality-soul development results in an elevated degree of God consciousness evidenced by character integrity and wisdom. We are approaching oneness with the Indwelling Spirit.

Because of the dual motivation of our animal drives and spiritual leadings, inner conflict and ambivalence is inevitable. What we are today is not so important as the direction in which we are facing and what we are striving to become. With our cooperation, the Spirit is the sure victor in this struggle. We should never lose sight of the evolutionary nature of human growth and development. As we strive for a harmonious, holistic integration of physical systems, mental-emotional systems, and social-environmental systems, our spiritual development is greatly facilitated.

Throughout the entire process of personality development our mind plays a key and determinative role. The mind is about the only universe entity which is subject to the will and control of the individual. It is in our psychological world that we live and move and fashion our being. We can twist, distort, and corrupt our minds with evil and sin or we can make them true, noble, and wise as we orient and harmonize them with spiritual reality.

Psychological discipline and control is the road to all human achievement. We need to build adequate intellectual and moral foundations before we can attain vocational and social competence and spiritual growth. Mind mastery through spirit dominance is the most important objective of human life. Everything else that is worthwhile follows. Character and achievement, civilization and culture, are products of the quality of our inner life.

When our physical life mechanism dies, our material body-mind ceases to function because we no longer have need of it. It has served as a necessary material scaffolding for the construction of a more enduring creation. Our identity and continuity, all that was of worth in our mortal life, has been transferred to our semispiritual soul and, under the care of the Father's Indwelling Spirit, we go on to greater adventures and education on a higher universe level where we will be given a more adequate body and mind to continue our ascendant career.

### *Summary Statement*

The field of operation for spiritual psychology is the human mind. Although our animal-origin body-mind is a passing phenomenon, it is the scaffolding which we use to build a more enduring Spirit-inspired edifice. Mind is the arena in which we now live and our hope for the future. Even though the human mind is limited and fallible, its potentials are entirely adequate for competent mortal living, identifying with Spirit reality, and cooperatively evolving an immortal soul. The objective of spiritual psychology is to actuate those mental processes whereby we master our minds through the dominance of spiritual values, making them noble, wise, and loving.

## 7. Planetary Realities: The Total Ecological Environment

We live in a total ecological environment which has physical, social, cultural, and spiritual aspects. Land and water, atmosphere and stratosphere, soil and micro-organisms, plants and animals, the earth and all of its inhabitants, live together in intradependent and interdependent relationships. These dependencies may be intimate and immediate or distant and cumulative. Our planet is an ecosystem where everything exists in relation to everything else. These organismic influences may be symbiotic or antagonistic.

Selfish, egocentric, and exploitive relationships with people and natural resources are ultimately self-defeating and suicidal. They eventuate in evil, sin, suffering, and unhappiness. Cooperative, conserving, appreciative, synergistic, and loving relationships among people and natural resources are germane to spiritual development and growth. Although the inner world of the mind and the outer world of the environment are quite different, they can be harmonized through spiritual insight and human wisdom.

Human beings are not created to live in isolation; we have a constant need for the stimulation and support of companionship. All that is of worth in society and culture has its roots in the family and small group relationships. While cultural evolution is the product of the inner world of the mind and spirit, its augmentation is dependent on creative leadership and the wise structuring of social institutions.

In critical socioeconomic situations moral power and spiritual energy make the difference between the breakdown of government and the stability and growth of the social, economic, and political structures. Vibrant faith in the truths of the Father/Motherhood of God and the brother/sisterhood of all people will progressively lift world civilization to higher and higher levels of spiritual culture. Religion, a first-hand experience of God, is designed to change and master the environment. A static, second-hand religion, however, is dominated by its environment. Whenever and wherever humankind has had living faith in spiritual realities, they have transformed their society and their environment.

As a planet and as individuals we live, move, and have our being in the immanence of the Supreme. Indeed, the entire universe is an ecological, responsive, living organism. As the German philosopher Hegel envisioned, the cosmos functions as an integrated system. Universe laws are directed by supreme intelligence circuits; the energy lanes of space nourish the material creation; and the evolutionary overcontrol of an all-wise Regulator keeps the universe in dynamic, creative tension designed to accomplish the loving purposes of Supreme fulfillment for all creation. We live in a friendly, supportive universe which is controlled by an infinitely wise and loving Universal Father.

### *Summary Statement*

We live in a total ecological environment which has physical, social, cultural, and spiritual aspects. The entire universe is an ecological, responsive, living organism. Selfish, egocentric, and exploitive relationships with people and natural resources are ultimately self defeating and suicidal. We exist in a friendly, supportive universe which is controlled by an infinitely wise and loving Universal Father.

The seven basic realities of experience must be recognized, acknowledged, and reasonably understood before spiritual-psychological activities can be effective. They are the context in which the principles of spiritual psychology function. The truths in our relationship with these realities are permanent; the facts associated with our understanding of these foundation stones of experience are undergoing constant and progressive change.

* * *

## B.

## THE SEVEN KEY DETERMINERS
## (The Becoming Conditions)

### 1. Spiritual Resources: Spirit Ministry and Spirit Gravity

We human beings, as we live our lives in the habiliments of the flesh, are all too conscious of our earthiness and vulnerability. We need constantly to remind ourselves of who we are: mortal sons and daughters of God. But even more, we should be aware of the marvelous spiritual ministry which has been provided for us. We are guided and undergirded by a three-fold spirit ministry which was discussed in the first section of this primer. Let us briefly review this divine shepherding that undergirds all creation and is the foundation of spiritual psychology.

A spark or fragment of the Universal Father's spirit indwells the human mind. The Indwelling Spirit is our constant companion, leading us in the direction of timeless reality, transcendent beauty, and transforming love. The Spirit of Truth surrounds us, making

God the Son real in our experience and sensitizing us to the liberating insights of truth. The ministry of God the Spirit stimulates us with the presence of the Holy Spirit, which nourishes our minds with the cosmic enlightenment of the ennobling will of the Father and the healing ways of the Son. This triune ministry is perfectly unified and we psychologically experience it as one.

We are, additionally, attracted and drawn to Ultimate Reality by a three-fold spirit-gravity system. Just as material bodies are attracted by physical gravity, the soul and superconscious aspect of mind are drawn by spirit gravity. The Father's personality-gravity circuit pulls all personalities toward his will and presence. The Son's spirit-gravity circuit stimulates spiritual growth. The more we evolve spiritually, the greater pull this spirit gravity has upon us and the easier it is for us to produce the fruits of the spirit. God the Spirit is the source of the mind-gravity circuit. The cosmic mind draws all spirit-related mind qualities toward the Infinite Spirit and generates God consciousness. This triune spirit gravity is perfectly coordinated, pulling us toward truth, beauty, and goodness, God's will and way, and is psychologically experienced as a unified influence.

Over and above this gracious and replete ministry provided by the persons of the Paradise Trinity, there is the overcontrol of providence assuring the progressive spiritual development of all personalities who dedicate themselves to the doing of the Father's will. Much of what we consider providential in the escape from suffering or the blessing of unearned wealth or pleasure is not the result of divine action but is the product of our own imagination and the fortuitous juxtaposition of the circumstances of chance. Such unearned good fortune may actually be an impediment to growth, while the apparent cruelty of tribulation and suffering may in reality be the tempering fire which anneals the soft and immature personality into the tempered steel of real character. Authentic providence determines that all things, both good and evil, eventually work together for the spiritual growth and salvation of all God-knowing and faithful people.

In the midst of this rich endowment of divine downreach, it is not surprising that there is a reality in religious experience which is unassailable and incontrovertible. This reality response of spiritual experience is a cosmic endowment which transcends reason, philosophy, science, and all other human achievements. While it may be confirming and comforting to engage in the rigors of philosophic logic and coherence which demonstrate the reasonableness of faith in the existence of God, or to observe the scientific evidence for the symbiotic, synergistic, and teleological nature of the material world, these are second-order psychological experiences. For the mind which has no first-hand experience of God, there are no convincing intellectual proofs for his existence. Those minds which have already intuited this reality presence or ground of being need no other evidence to exercise faith. Faith starts from mustard-seed beginnings.

If we are to grow as individuals or as a culture we need to be open to divine guidance. Every individual goes through different phases of growth and development which require the corrective discipline of wise spiritual attunement. Each new generation should have a fresh restatement of the timeless truths of the kingdom of God to facilitate a creative adjustment to the ever-new material, social, and spiritual problems of living. Our Indwelling Guide can often contribute new spiritual insights through the channels of controlled imagination as we search for truth and strive to free ourselves from preconceived opinions and long-standing prejudices.

The static concepts of theology are intellectual formulations which, without the undergirding of spiritual power, cannot reach the motivational depth to change lives or transform behavior. It is the Spirit that quickens; only a vital spiritual relationship with the source of all creativity can bring life to these dead intellectual shibboleths. Unless and until the divine Spirit empowers these formulations of truth, those who preach or teach them are little more than intellectual parrots and rubber stamps of authority and tradition.

We must learn to step aside from our institutional and vocational routines, from the daily rush of life, to refresh the soul, inspire the mind, and renew the spirit through prayer and worship. Prayer and worship are complementary. Prayer has an element of self-interest or social-personal concern; but it may lead to worship. Worship is the contemplation of God, self-forgetting, and an end in itself. It is the part identifying with the whole. Worship is the greatest privilege and most creative activity of humankind. It inspires service and is the foundation of the highest joys experienced by human beings. This psychological adoration and identification with the Source of all things and beings stimulates soul growth, stabilizes the mind, and integrates personality.

Prayer is fellowship with God which enlarges insight. It is both a sound psychological practice which augments self-realization and an effective spiritual technique to expand the soul. Seeking divine guidance is not a substitute for human ingenuity and action, nor a way in which to escape life's difficulties, but a means of mental-spiritual empowerment to face conflict and suffering meaningfully and courageously. Prayer does not change God but it may alter the person praying and it unfailingly enlarges the soul's receptivity capacity. It is a mental-spiritual methodology for changing that which is into that which ought to be.

Immature prayer attempts to plead or bargain with God for health, wealth, power, or preference. Prayer, however, cannot be used to circumvent universe laws. We should pray for divine guidance to solve our human problems, not for some cosmic or miraculous solution. Our spiritual level is revealed by the nature of our concerns and petitions. Words are not important in prayer; God responds to the true and sincere attitudes of the mind and soul.

To pray effectively we must face reality honestly and intelligently, attempt to solve problems creatively through spiritual guidance with the resources we have, be dedicated to doing the will of God, and have living faith. Our fellowship with God should be unselfish, identifying with and loving all of his children. We must be honest and sincere and see that our aspirations and supplications are harmonious with our highest insights and most comprehensive knowledge. And they should be offered with complete submission to the Father's all-wise will. This personal relationship with God is indispensable to spiritual growth and a major resource in developing personality effectiveness and inner peace. Such God-knowing people are never alone even when isolated from human association.

Prayers are answered according to the degree of their spiritual content, intent, and wisdom. Selfish and materialistic petitions do not enter the spirit circuits; they are as "sounding brass and tinkling cymbals." They may, however, bring comfort and hope to the person praying and they increase the soul's growth potential. Much of the change effected by prayer and worship takes place on an unconscious level and becomes operative in our lives through action and service. The leading of the Indwelling Spirit is so benign, subtle, and unimposing, so admixed with the ordinary things of life, that we subjectively cannot be certain whether our inclinations have their origin in our subconscious motivational needs or our superconscious spiritual guidance.

Strong emotional feelings are not a sure sign of the leading of our Indwelling Spirit. Intense affective desire is a characteristic expression of thwarted subconscious needs. Neither should we confuse conscience with divine guidance. Conscience is the psychological product of our training and social conditioning. Probably the greatest danger in evaluating inner experience is to mistake mystical and psychic states in which we hear voices or see visions for divine communications or revelation. Such experiences are most impressive but may originate from psychic or even psychotic episodes. Subjective experience which is not critically examined and evaluated has often resulted in radical movements and religious fanaticism.

Those who are aware of the self-deceptive capacities of the human mind are not likely to declare "God told me to...." All inner guidance should be carefully evaluated before assuming it is spiritual direction. It is less dangerous to ignore or depart from divine guidance in the assumption that such inner direction is only our own personal inclination than to mistake our human ideas and desires for the will of God.

Our inner orientation should be tested by objective standards as well as subjective evaluation. Is it harmonious with the highest thinking and values of human culture? Does this way of life clash with scientifically verified facts? What do the people whose judgment I most respect think about it? How does time and experience affect this leading or sense of mission? After we are confident that the idea or action we are contemplating is good and consistent with the highest and best that we know, it is time to get experiential validation—we need to act.

What kind of feedback does experience give us? Does this way of life undergird health and improve our mental functioning? Does it promote love and unity or instigate fear, anger, and disharmony? If our service or ministry arouses fear and conflict, is it associated with the frustration and pain of growth or the suffering inherent in that which is destructive and evil? Is our appreciation of truth, beauty, and goodness enhanced? Does this life style and faith increase God consciousness and lead people closer to God?

Experience gives us information and wisdom which thinking and theory alone cannot reveal. With this testing of our "inner leadings" by thought and action we make decisions and shape our lives. We then should live in the deep conviction that we are perceiving the will of God to the best of our abilities as we are striving to follow the highest and best that we know. It is balance which characterizes spiritual wisdom. As our personalities achieve the symmetry of the balanced unification of physical, mental, and spiritual powers, the greatest amount of light and truth can be mediated to us.

Our spiritual resources have unlimited potential to furnish us guidance and undergird our lives. The divine purpose for human life is to evolve our souls so that we have survival potential and can be resurrected on a higher universe level where our more advanced spiritual education will begin. Those whose lives are directed by a sense of calling even now have a transcendental quality to their mortal careers. As we strive to actualize the Indwelling Spirit's plan for our lives, our efforts are augmented and ennobled by this divine-human partnership. The limits of human potential are expanded when incorporated with divine purpose. When we dedicate all that we have to the service of God, then our humanness merges with divine possibilities.

### *Summary Statement*

The power of spiritual psychology is the threefold ministry of the Trinity. It is replete and invincible. The Spirit quickens, renews, and transforms. Nothing can substitute for a first-hand experience of God; it is unassailable and incontrovertible, transcending reason, philosophy, and science. Prayer is a sound psychological practice which undergirds living and expands the soul. Inner guidance, however, should be thoroughly evaluated to confirm its spiritual quality. Worship is identifying with God—Ultimate Truth, Beauty, and Goodness; it is the most creative activity of human beings.

✳ ✳ ✳

## 2. Guiding Supports: Facts, Meanings, and Values

The basic forms of universe reality—matter, mind, and spirit—are experienced in the cognitive form of things, meanings, and values and give rise to the disciplines of science, philosophy, and religion. The gathering and accumulation of the facts of knowledge takes place at the scientific level of intellectual activity. The study of the relationships, meaning, and validity of knowledge is a philosophic function which yields wisdom. Experiencing the spiritual reality of truth, dedicating oneself to follow the Indwelling Spirit's guidance, living by faith, and producing the beauty and goodness of the fruits of the Spirit are germane to the practice of religion. Human existence involves the use of reason and wisdom to integrate fact, truth, and faith in experience. The quality of our lives is determined in large part by the accuracy of our scientific facts, the coherence of our philosophic insights, and the reality-centeredness of our religious values.

### Sources and Types of Knowledge

We have three basic sources of knowledge: perception of the material world, information inherent in the nature of the human mind or consciousness, and value perception. This three-fold base of knowledge is interrelated in endless complexity. Any understanding of experience which does not take into consideration all of these sources of knowledge invariably becomes distorted. Spiritual growth is related to the mental expansion afforded by the sources of knowledge.

Religious progress is stimulated by the exercise of curiosity and the love of adventure, the coordination of abilities in self-realization, and a sense of humility which motivates the hunger for knowledge and wisdom.

The content of the human mind is largely the result of our perception of the physical world. As material beings having five basic senses which provide forms of physiological sensation, along with minds which operate through the material brain, the bulk of our experience centers around empirical knowledge. This tangible set of data has the advantage of being objective, having common verifiability, and lending itself readily to quantitation. Science is rooted in our empirical perception. Science, however, is handicapped by the limitations of material reality; therefore, it is possible to be empirically correct in our fact observations but wrong in our truth judgments.

The nature and quality of our minds determines the form and limitations of both empirical and spiritual perception. The inherent characteristics of the human mind designate the patterns and categories in which sense data are ordered and organized and the reality quality of our value insights. Those authentic and verifiable cognitive capacities which we posses by virtue of the nature of the human mind are known as rational abilities. Some types of rational thought are relatively independent of specific forms of empirical perception. Such inherent rational knowledge is referred to as a priori or noëtic perception. One of the categories of a priori knowledge, for instance, is the "law of noncontradiction," which states that two contradictory propositions cannot both be true.

Rational perception has the advantage of being applicable to both empirical and spiritual knowledge. It links and integrates facts and values in experience. Mathematics, logic, and reason are useful tools of both science and religion. Rational knowledge by itself, however, tends to end in sterile abstractions or crystallize into static concepts which often hinder human progress. Its rigid and circumscribed theories and dogmas usually have a limited correlation with living material and spiritual reality. Only as empirical observations make it relevant to existential problems, and value judgments direct it toward the great goals of human existence, does rational knowledge achieve its highest expression.

Value perception largely determines the quality and goals of human life. Our perceptions of truth, beauty, and goodness contribute a spiritual dimension to life. Just as our object or fact cognition is the product of matter-mind interaction, so our value perceptions are the result of spirit-mind interaction. The deeper aspects of value awareness, like the nuclear world of matter, must be studied by inference as our direct consciousness of spiritual reality is extremely limited.

Creative, spirit-actualizing people seem to have superior value insight, which has the advantage of perceiving key factors in our empirical-rational experience and relating them in ways which bring optimum good to human life. Spiritual knowledge by itself, however, is subject to distortion and illusion. Both objective and subjective knowledge are fallible. We must constantly test our value insights by rational analysis and empirical experience. True values are never irrational nor out of harmony with scientific fact, although they usually transcend both rational thought and empirical evidence.

It is important to remember that all of our sources of knowledge are interdependent. The single-eyed materialistic scientist, intellectual rationalist, and religious mystic are unable to correctly visualize and adequately comprehend the depth of universe reality. Truth may be handicapped, but not invalidated, by its association with distorted science or obsolete theology. It can undergird human experience even when linked with inaccurate facts and erroneous thinking. When both science and religion become less narrow and dogmatic, philosophy will be able to achieve a more unified comprehension of the universe. As fact, truth, and value are more holistically understood, great strides can be made in spiritual growth. In developmental experience we normally proceed from facts, to meanings, and then to values. Accordingly, in the hierarchical emphasis of human culture, science gives way to philosophy and philosophy eventually recognizes the priority of spiritual experience and Spirit Reality.

The limitations of the mortal mind and the evolving nature of reality make all human knowledge relative. As the body of knowledge enlarges, the frontier of the unknown has a concurrent expansion. Truth, itself, is relative and expanding, achieving new expression in every generation and in each person. Nevertheless, human knowledge is generally dependable. As we make decisions and take action on the basis of our most reliable information, we gradually acquire wisdom. Our behavior becomes more and more harmonious with existential reality.

## Popular Tests for Truth

Over centuries of experience we have followed various uncritical pragmatic short cuts to the discovery of truth and the regulation of our behavior. One of the most common is making decisions on the basis of feeling-intuition. Following emotional inclinations is characteristic of immaturity. Feelings all too often are determined by misinformation, illusions, and defense mechanisms with their endless forms of unconscious and irrational motivation. The Indwelling Spirit makes contact with our lives, not through feelings and emotions, but in the highest realms of superconscious, spiritualized thinking.

Whenever we as individuals feel threatened by our egocentric behavior, we often retreat into the security of the customs and mores of our society. Although group opinion tends to be more balanced and inclusive than our individual inclinations, it is subject to all of the distortions of selective perception, emotional illusion, and irrational assumption which characterize uncritical individual feelings and actions. The customs and mores of the culture, while bringing stability to society, are even greater barriers to moral and spiritual growth than individual prejudice and ignorance. These folkways achieve a spurious validity through mass approval and sometimes precipitate atrocities in the name of social or religious justice.

During the millenniums of the historical process contemporary societies experienced instability, mass suffering, and social crisis. In these critical periods prophetic leaders arise, pointing to "the wisdom of the fathers" as the road to recover and prosperity.

These touchstones of antiquity—sacred scriptures, wise sayings of great leaders, or courageous acts of martyred heroes—become the guiding standards of society. Thus tradition and authority establish themselves as the arbiter of all behavior and belief. The experience of the centuries is an excellent test of human knowledge and values. Over the years, society does acquire wisdom. But along with this wisdom is associated much that is nonessential, illusory, and erroneous. Truths, half-truths, misconceptions, and the literary-cultural forms in which they are communicated are hopelessly confused. And contemporary situations always contain new and unique conditions for which traditional wisdom is not applicable.

Since we cannot become experts in many fields, we must depend upon knowledgeable people of integrity to advise us in almost every area of life. Authority, therefore, is the pragmatic short cut to truth most widely accepted by society. The use of expert opinion becomes so generalized in a complex society that the conventional mind assumes authority to be an adequate criterion of truth. This assumption is obviously fallacious. Even when experts give us the most reliable information available, the perceptive individual will always realize that the judgment given is not true because an authority declared it to be true but because they are referring to sources of validation which other adequately trained persons could confirm.

When this valid social basis for the use of expert opinion is forgotten or placed in a secondary position, authoritarianism results. This intellectual bigotry cripples growth in all fields of knowledge. The history of all scholarly disciplines demonstrates that often the only way new ideas or discoveries are accepted is when the old experts or authorities die off. It is an ironic paradox of life that authority, while being the most useful short cut to reliable knowledge, when corrupted into authoritarianism, is in a position farthest removed from an adequate philosophic criterion of truth. Dependence on the use of tradition and authority is a common weakness of conservative minds.

Religious authoritarianism is a major impediment to spiritual growth. There is a great temptation for religious institutions to substitute historic fact and sectarian authority for spiritual truth in their theology. Zealous and pragmatic religionists translate high spiritual truths into specific rules of living whose legalistic format is devoid of the spiritual truth and power which inspired their formulation. The comprehension of truth frees one from all legalistic rule slavery and welcomes us to the supreme liberty of living by spiritual principles.

## Critical Tests for Truth

There are three approaches to the critical evaluation of the validity of facts, meanings, and values: the scientific method of fact validity, the philosophical method of coherence validity; and the religious method of intuited truth. All three tests utilize all of the sources of knowledge but each emphasizes one facet of reality.

The main steps of the scientific method are: observation, hypothesis, experimental design, experimentation, evaluation, and verification. It is intersensual and intersubjective; objectivity is of fundamental importance. The observational aspect of the scientific method is rooted in our empirical perception potentials.

Rational procedures of both deduction and induction are important scientific tools. Mere correlation, workability, or association is not an adequate criterion to establish a cause-and-effect relationship. Rational thought is also basic in the areas of experimental design, control, and evaluation. Value perception largely determines the area which is investigated, and creative insight is primarily responsible for the nature of the projected hypothesis. Value insight also plays a significant role in evaluating experimental evidence. All of the human knowledge sources and capacities used by scientists function adequately only in a composite, holistic unity. Because of the objective nature of the scientific method, there is general agreement in its results.

A more comprehensive test of validity is furnished by the philosophic method of coherence in evaluating meanings. The coherence method is dialectical but it is a reasoning process rooted in the three primary sources of perceptual knowledge. The philosopher considers our total empirical-scientific knowledge but does not identify validity completely with scientific facts. Philosophers use the highest forms of rational thought but do not confuse authenticity with mere logical validity. The coherence method uses our total capacity for creative thinking and value comprehension but does not equate veracity simply with mystical or intuitive insight. Our highest philosophical wisdom is achieved when our total knowledge is weighed and evaluated in a dialectical process which culminates in relevant decisions. The philosophical method does not bring uniformity of opinion because each person's mind and experience is different and therefore differential weights are given to the basic sources of knowledge. It does, however, tend to make for unity in the philosophic quest because common sources of knowledge and cognitive disciplines are recognized and used.

The ultimate human approach to reality is the religious method of intuited truth. Those who hunger for spiritual knowledge and growth will search for truth and divine guidance (Ultimate Reality). Knowledge is a mindal attainment which has the restrictions of finite experience; truth is a spiritual reality perception which transcends intellectual limitations. The truth insight of the soul reinforces philosophical reasoning. Intuitive spiritual sensitivity creates visions of truth which faith undergirds and transmutes into living reality. Truth is dominant in the spiritually endowed mind. Over and above the facts and reason which govern our daily lives, we intuit glimpses of spiritual reality and supreme values. Our noëtic experience of truth, beauty, and goodness is superior to all other knowledge in directing our lives. It is the foundation upon which faith is established and developed. It is personal experience with the Truth, the Way, and the Life.

Human beings, however, have no infallible way to distinguish between intuited truth and other forms of inner knowledge and direction; therefore, all of our feelings, attitudes, and actions should be checked and verified by coherent philosophical reasoning and scientific facts. The final test of truth is experience. As experience builds faith in the spiritual foundations of the universe, we are able to face defeat, suffering, and the unknown future with courage and great confidence.

Truth is a dynamic, living spiritual reality. It transcends knowledge and other purely material levels of reality. Truth cannot be captured or defined by words but can be known through living experience. Because human beings are Spirit indwelt, we can know truth, live the truth, experience the growth of truth in the soul, and enjoy its liberating influence on the mind; but truth cannot be imprisoned in creeds, dogmas, or theology. Truth can be transmitted from person to person through interpersonal communication, but when we attempt to place living truth in impersonal, static forms such as the written or printed word, which is material in nature, it is downstepped to the intellectual level of human knowledge or wisdom. Truth is then diluted from living spiritual power into its material intellectual shadow. Only dead truth can be captured in theological concepts. In this way religious experience is reduced to religious philosophy.

It is possible for a person reading this static or dead truth to either assimilate it at the intellectual knowledge level or experientially transform it back again into truth—living spiritual power. Both knowledge and truth have a place in human life; they are complementary. Physicians, however, do not confuse living human beings with the static nature of cadavers. Likewise, religionists should not equate the dead formulas of theology with the living power of truth. But just as the practice of medicine is greatly assisted by the dissection of cadavers, so the analytical study of the static forms of truth in theology can be of immense value to the living practice of religion.

There are two basic types of religious experience. Those religious activities based on fear, emotion, tradition, institution building, and theology are intellectual-humanistic religious functions. Those religious devotions centered in personal experience and fellowship with the Indwelling Spirit of the Universal Father and the actualization of the fruits of the spirit in daily living are spiritual-divine religious expressions. Intellectual religion is dominated by a second-hand knowledge of God, theological beliefs, and institutional service. Spiritual religion is motivated by a first-hand experience of God, living faith, and service to humanity wherever you are and in whatever occupation you may find yourself. The one emphasizes the intellectualization or indoctrination of dead forms of truth which have been stepped down to aspects of human knowledge or wisdom; the other lives by spiritual truth which is spontaneous, dynamic, and creative in its expression in human personality. All planetary religions are a mixture of humanistic and divine religious orientations. Each individual expresses a unique combination of these forms of religious experience.

### *Summary Statement*

Spiritual psychology is guided and validated by the basic sources of knowledge. Facts, meanings, and values are interrelated in human experience. Failure to include any of these sources of reality invariably distorts the outcome of thought and action. The materialist, the rationalist, and the mystic do not comprehend the depth of universe reality. All human knowledge is relative but reasonably dependable.

Popular tests for truth are lacking in validity. The critical scientific, philosophic, and religious evaluations of truth are all necessary and interdependent. Truth has a dynamic, living spiritual quality which cannot be captured by impersonal language and creeds. Religious experience is a combination of intellectual-humanistic functions and spiritual-divine experience. Spiritual psychology deals primarily with personal spiritual experience. This is the only religious experience with a direct relationship with Ultimate Reality having the power to transform life and society.

* * *

## 3. Human Determiners: Will and Mind Mastery

The human will is the key determiner of mortal destiny. Although finite volition is limited, we have sufficient freedom of will to identify with values and shape our mental orientation and growth. Because of the self limitation of God, his Indwelling Spirit is always subservient to our will. We have the opportunity to identify with reality and survive our mortal experience or to disassociate ourselves from truth, beauty, and goodness and terminate our existence. When we dedicate ourselves to following the will of God, we have embarked on the road to salvation.

Such a choice is not a surrender of will but a recognition of reality. It is an enlightenment, an expansion, and a glorification of will through our highest truth insights. It is a consecration of will in identifying with the Indwelling Spirit of God. Spiritual growth involves a progressive identification with God. The goal of mortal destiny is the eventual final and complete attunement of our will with the will of God. At this moment of perfect harmony there is a fusion, a oneness, a permanent bonding of the human and the divine.

Our will determines our motivational identities and these consistent ideals shape our growth and achievement. Every decision opens new possibilities in human experience and a fresh capacity for growth. Character is established not only by critical decisions but by the number, frequency, and persistence of decisions resulting in consistent constructive attitudes and behavior. Our lives are directed not so much by our theoretical and theological beliefs as through our judgmental determinations, decisions, and steadfast faith.

Half-hearted decisions are really not decisions at all; they are wishful thinking. Such partial devotion to truth, justice, or virtue is ineffective and insufficient to actualize personal spiritual growth. Only wholehearted decisions and decisive consecration will serve as the catalysts to master the limitations of human nature and evolve personality potentials into the reality of spiritual power.

Life is a process of becoming. The important thing is not where we are now but the direction in which we are facing and striving. We cannot escape the responsibility of self-determination. Following the line of least resistance or failing to make life-altering decisions is itself a latent decision, an abrogation of responsibility. All of us have a certain range of freedom of choice which we may exercise. The Indwelling Spirit and the spiritual forces of the universe will lead and point the way when we listen for guidance but they never coerce us in decision making. We are allowed to go the way of our own inclinations or choosing.

The direction of personality growth and human achievement is categorically placed in the power potentials of the individual will. The great adventure of mortal existence is the transit from experience centered in the animal legacy of the material mind to living by the spiritual dynamics of superconscious insight and the inner peace and joy of soul consciousness. This transformation is brought about by the creative force and unswerving constancy of our personality decisions which, in essence, affirm: "It is my will that your will be done." Our minds have the capacity to translate the values of the Spirit into meanings of intelligence; our volition has the power to actualize, to concretize, these value meanings into living realities.

The direction and control of our minds, our thinking processes, is basic to self-discipline and spiritual growth. Mind mastery is one of the most important of all human accomplishments. By will decision we accept or reject and redirect the thoughts that come to us and thereby influence the content of consciousness and the ultimate quality of our minds. The nature of our consciousness, our thoughts, determine what we become, our quality of being.

Through the constant and repeated discipline of our thoughts, bringing them in harmony with our highest concepts of truth, beauty, and goodness, we eventually condition and shape our feelings through gradual change or through the instant transformation of spiritual insight. Emotional maturity is an accompanying condition or prerequisite of spiritual growth. Significant change, therefore, cannot be accomplished by mere force of will. Growth always requires time and reality foundations. Before we can dominate and redirect the drives and incentives of our lower animal nature we must, through the techniques of will and mind direction, build a solid appreciation and interest in, and love for, those spiritual values which undergird the higher and more idealistic conduct which we desire.

Pleasure is a good and legitimate human experience but it is not an end in itself. It is designed to accompany and reinforce reality-oriented activities. But self-gratification can easily be distorted into egocentric goals. Undisciplined pleasure seeking destroys both the individual and society. We need to direct our energies and restrain our sensuality. The deepest hunger of our authentic self cannot be satisfied by physical pleasures. Rugged and intelligent self-control is the master expediter of human virtue and it is achieved through will directives and mind mastery.

Will is that aspect of mind which enables our subjective consciousness to aspire to be Godlike. When we strive to harmonize our will with the will of the Universal Father we are psychologically in the kingdom of heaven. It is the motive that is all important. When our motive is not pure, subtle rationalizations ease us surreptitiously on the road to falsehood and evil. The morality of any decision or action is determined by its motive. When our intent is to be loyal to the highest truth we know, the will of God as we understand it, our behavior is ethical. The mistakes we make are then errors of the mind, not of the heart.

As we grow spiritually, the pleasures of truth, beauty, and service become dominant in our lives. Spiritual reality guides and shapes our total personality through the mediation of mind. Mind mastery is a slow but sure process when we dedicate ourselves to follow the Indwelling Spirit's guidance. Through cognitive spiritual dominance our minds are integrated and balanced. We experience the inner healing power of faith and all of our activities are more effective. Trustworthiness and responsibility characterize our relationships. Our will dedication and mind transformation evolve the soul. Those who are thus born of the spirit are indomitable; they are challenged by difficulties, stimulated by the unknown, and invigorated by opposition.

### *Summary Statement*

The major determiners, the rudders, of spiritual psychology are will decisions and mind mastery. We cannot escape the responsibility of self-determination. Our will decisions establish our goals and purposes; the control and mastery of our minds fashion the resources and power available for the achievement of our objectives. Spiritual foundations must be built before urges, drives, and emotions can be directed and specific accomplishments are possible. Half-hearted efforts are nonavailing; only whole-hearted decisions and decisive consecration can summon the spiritual resources for soul growth. Such spirit-born character is master of the material scene.

* * *

## 4. Emotional Actualizers: Faith, Courage, and Love

Thought and emotion are closely related. It is possible for emotion to dominate thought and for thinking to control emotion. Through the process of mind mastery we also determine the primary emotions which color and energize our consciousness. The negative emotions such as fear, anxiety, and doubt are usually associated with deficiency needs and the positive emotions such as optimism, joy, and love tend to accompany creative and self-actualizing needs. All of our emotions have a place in our survival and growth struggles, but the most constructive aspects of life are promoted by the positive emotions. The Indwelling Spirit fosters the dominance of the self-actualizing emotions, the greatest of which are faith, courage, and love.

### Faith

Faith is the ground cognitive-affective activity which actualizes spiritual growth. It goes beyond empirical knowledge, yet it is rooted in first-hand reality experience. Faith is spiritual, creative, and dynamic. It is the essence of spiritualized creative imagination and aspiration. Belief is intellectual in nature and is static, exclusive, and confining. Faith evolves and liberates; belief tends to fixate and enslave. Belief can be encapsulated in words, statements, and dogmas. Faith transcends concepts and definitions; it is experienced and lived. Faith must be personal and originates from within. Belief is only an intellectual acceptance of certain theological-cultural concepts which usually are perpetuated as group possessions.

Belief is transmuted to the spiritual level of faith when it becomes the ground motivation of our lives and determines the way we live. Faith does not abandon intelligence and reason nor fear critical examination. It is predicated on our most reliable facts, highest meanings, and ultimate values. Faith, nevertheless, is not dependent on worldly knowledge, human wisdom, or the sophistication of social culture; it can guide and sustain the most humble and unlearned of human beings.

Faith has the quality of spiritual assurance. It delivers us from fear, anxiety, and crippling conflict. Those who are sure about ultimates are not intimidated by the contemporary. If we have living faith we are not overwhelmed by disappointment, defeat, injustice, or suffering. We see beyond current limitations and conditions and know that God's Indwelling Spirit will not only sustain us in whatever may befall us, but the Father's creative guidance will bring positive and constructive reactions and experiences out of the tragic and terrible events of mortal existence. Those who know they are sons and daughters of God do not allow material difficulties to stand in the way of soul growth and spiritual development.

## Courage

Courage is the outgoing, adventurous attitude of those who are willing to call upon the potentials of their resources in facing the problems and challenges of living. It is an indigenous endowment of creature mind. Since all growth involves pain and suffering, courage is an elemental requirement of development and learning. New insights and meanings become clear only amid stress and conflict. Those who do not have the courage to be, to actualize their potentialities, will remain emotional, intellectual, and spiritual dwarfs. Spiritual help does not come to those who refuse to take action within the potentials of their own abilities. We do not grow until we overcome indolence, evasion, half-hearted efforts, and the tendency to follow the path of least resistance. Our abilities and capabilities are enlarged when we have the courage to push ourselves to limits. Nothing of worth and real accomplishment is easy. Some of our greatest failures occasionally become the source of our greatest experiential blessings. Frustration, stress, and tribulation are the tempering fires of experience which build strong character.

Courage, however, may become distorted into pride and egotism when it is not conditioned by faith, wisdom, and love. Discretion often is the better part of valor. Development is an evolutionary process which requires that solid experiential foundations must be established before new and enlarged responsibilities are safely undertaken. One of the best antidotes to defuse our illusions of self-importance and pride is a healthy sense of humor.

The highest form of courage is spiritual. Such fortitude is born with our identification with Ultimate Reality. Confidence and self-esteem are birthrights of the children of God. When we see ourselves as sons or daughters of the Creator, we realize the forces of the universe are on our side. As we identify with ultimate universe values, we are confident that actions inspired by these spiritual realities will eventually prevail.

Courage is the personal-spiritual attitude which affirms and proclaims those facts and values by which we live. It largely establishes the surety and rate of our spiritual growth and character acquirement. Courage enables us to carry on in the presence of frustration and failure, to live with hope and confidence in the face of seemingly unsolvable human problems, and to realize that even when the structures of civilization crash there is an inner citadel of the soul which is unassailable. When pushed beyond the limits of our own resources and capacities, spiritually enlightened courage tells us that even though we are unable to cope, there dwells within us one who can and will come to our rescue. Courage is the essence of victorious spiritual living.

## Love

Love determines the quality and effectiveness of spiritual living. It is the master spiritual attitude which acts as a synergistic catalyst and integrates all of the spiritual qualities of human personality. Love enlarges and unifies the power of the soul and is our nearest approach to Godlike behavior. It is the supreme reality of the universe, the most helpful guide to truth insight, and the greatest relationship between and among personalities.

On the material level, love appears to be a naive and unrealistic method of pursuing political objectives or establishing social justice. Brute force and material power do determine events at the physical level of existence. For this reason spiritually immature individuals and societies must be regulated and controlled by physical power. But as civilization develops, those who have the vision and the courage to sacrifice privilege, and even life, in acts of love for truth and justice slowly shift the locus of power among people and nations.

Spiritual reality through the mediation of mental influence gradually becomes dominant over physical power. In this way love, the cardinal spiritual power, triumphs in individual and planetary life. Just as the principle of the conservation of energy rules the physical continuum, so the law of the conservation of goodness dominates spiritual reality. An act of love and goodness is never totally lost. Because of the supremacy of spiritual reality, our decisions and actions are potent and efficacious in proportion to the goodness, truth, and love of their motivation.

Anger is a behavioral index and measure of our lack of spiritual orientation and control. Usually people do not wish to be harmful; and when they do hurtful things, they believe they are justified in their actions. Our first reaction to angry remarks or actions should be to ask ourselves, where and why is this person hurting? If we make an effort to ascertain the deeper motives, it is easier to understand and love. When we view other people as the Universal Father's children, and love them as persons, even while disagreeing with their behavior, we can forgive.

Forgiveness, however, does not relieve the person from responsibility for his or her actions. Love in an imperfect world is both an unconditional acceptance of the individual and a wise and disciplined response to the individual's behavior. Both mercy and justice must be considered. Tough love is not easy but it is always healing and helping. The most loving response to harmful and antisocial behavior is that action which has the greatest probability of stimulating personal and spiritual growth in the individual and good to society. The Spirit of Truth is ever leading us to wiser and more effective expressions of love. The actualization of love must be redefined on successive levels of spiritual growth as our material knowledge and truth insight are improved.

The leavening results of love are surprising and paradoxical revelations. When people know they are loved, things we could not predict or believe happen. Love is the atmosphere in which the fruits of the spirit flourish; it delivers us from the need for defensiveness and the protective veneers of artificiality. The Indwelling Spirit of God would lead us from the primitive reverence born of fear to the spiritually mature experience of love. Human greatness consists in a life permeated and dominated by love and motivated by a desire to live the truth of the will of God. Such a person will meet injustice with positive action, face the threats of violence by forbearance and love, and strive to overcome evil with good.

### *Summary Statement*

Faith, courage, and love are the dominant self-actualizing emotions of spiritual psychology. Faith is a spiritual attitude which is dynamic and undergirds life. Belief is an intellectual position which is static and void of spiritual power. Faith brings spiritual assurance and frees us from fear, anxiety, and crippling conflict. Courage is self-and universe-affirming confidence which is germane to all growth and learning. Love is the all-embracing spiritual attitude which acts as a synergistic catalyst for the self-actualizing emotions and motivations of human personality. It is our nearest approach to God-like behavior and the most powerful spiritual force in the universe. Spiritual psychology lives in these emotional actualizers of spiritual growth.

* * *

## 5. Required Conditions: Experience and Evolutionary Persistence

There are no substitutes for experience in life; nothing can take the place of a first-hand relationship with reality. Although the parameters of human potential are largely determined by biological inheritance, the level and quality of actual achievement is determined by our response to the vicissitudes of living. Experience is the reality continuum of mortal existence. Here we confront the determinants of destiny. Even though we are immersed in the physical constraints of living, our awareness of spiritual realities is the most significant shaper of the mortal adventure. God is the greatest of all human experiences. We are children of the Universal Father who has ordained that our spiritual growth shall be the product of a divine-human partnership. Through our truth, beauty, and goodness perception and will decisions we participate in the cocreation of ourselves. Experience is the cosmic cocoon of soul actualization.

We can learn much from history and the experience of others; however, the master teacher is personal experience. We learn by becoming involved with physical, mental, and spiritual realities. First-hand knowledge and wisdom are acquired by interaction with our environment, fellow human beings, and God. We grow by living and doing. Growth momentum is the law of experience. When inertia is overcome in any learning or development capacity, growth in this direction is augmented by past achievement and continued growth becomes increasingly spontaneous. As we struggle to overcome selfish tendencies, we become more concerned about the welfare of others and experience a greater urge to love them. This behavioral gravity applies to all forms of experience, including our decadence. As moral deterioration takes place in compliance with the motivation of evil and sin, it becomes easier to continue this slide into self-destruction.

Living relationships with reality should not be confused with intellectualization, imagination, or fantasy. Authentic experience is an involvement with physical and spiritual reality. It is a first-hand association with concrete aspects of the material world and a noëtic, personal relationship with the values of spiritual reality. When mental activity loses contact with these reality associations, it can be easily subverted into distortions and illusions.

Those whose lives are governed by fact and truth must ever distinguish the actual from the theoretical, doing from dreaming, and reality from illusion. Living is quite different from philosophizing about life. Faith, which is grounded in spiritual reality, can be distinguished from fantasy, which is the product of cognitive imagination, in that faith stimulates action and growth; whereas, fantasy is a psychological escape mechanism leading us to live in a dream world. Living in the present is reality oriented; dwelling on the past or daydreaming about future anticipations, while sometimes helpful and refreshing, is an invitation to reality evasion.

Truth retention and spiritual growth are related to the intensity and repetition of experience. Repeated experience is the sure road to knowledge assimilation and the ideal preparation for truth recognition. While insight is facilitated by stress and crisis involvement, growth takes place most creatively in the supportive atmosphere of love and freedom. Spiritual growth cannot be forced or coerced; it must come from within. When we hunger for truth, justice, or loving relationships we open ourselves to spiritual growth potentials.

Religion originates, and is centered in, personal value experience. It is the individual's total response, incorporated in behavioral rituals and lifestyles, to his or her understanding of ultimate values. The social ramifications of religious experience and the institutionalization of religion are second-order manifestations of personal experience. When an entire population is energized by a first-hand relationship with God, that society is irrepressibly creative. Authentic religion inspires action; living faith must *do* something about spiritual ideals. In a society where the great majority of people live by a second-hand religion, public welfare stagnates and progressively deteriorates.

True religious experience is dynamic and transforming. The intellectualization of religion in creeds, theology, and dogma translates spiritual truth and living faith into static human knowledge with all of the deficiencies and limitations of the material level of reality. This is why the prophets, who call people to a renewed relationship with God, have advanced spiritual growth; while the theologians, who intellectualize religion, along with the priests, who symbolize and ritualize faith, have arrested religious development.

Religious experience, therefore, should always supersede and dominate theology, for God can be known only through the realities of experience, not by instructing the mind. Theology may significantly enhance the faith of experience when she serves as the humble handmaiden of religion, not its proud, officious, orthodox judge and authority. Neither should material-bound symbols and rituals be substituted for living experience with the spiritual realities of the kingdom of God. They may, however, make this relationship with God more real and facilitate worship when they are not equated or confused with these spiritual realities.

The paramount requirement of religion is the experience of spiritual values, not thinking about theological concepts or philosophical theories. Intellectual ability, while most useful in solving material problems and assisting spiritual growth, is a second-class virtue when compared with spiritual values. The pride of intellectualism frequently blinds academic people to the limits of formal education. A loving mother may be able to give the best nurturant help to her children so that they are able to grow and develop in an ideal manner, yet utterly flunk an academic test in child psychology. In contrast, the most learned child psychologist may be a failure as a mother. Spiritual growth enables us to keep facts and truths in perspective.

The spiritual objective of religion is soul building, salvation. This is accomplished by establishing a living relationship, a partnership, with God. The kingdom of God in its vertical nature is an individual, loving, personal relationship with God; in its horizontal nature it is loving service to our fellow human beings. When the purpose of religion is distorted into the service of religious institutions or any other form of religious totalitarianism, religious humanism and socialism have taken the place of the spiritual kingdom of God.

Spiritual growth requires a special quality of religious experience. It demands evolutionary persistence. Human beings start life as helpless babes with an animal legacy far removed from the challenges of spiritual growth. Difficulty, pain, and suffering, therefore, play a significant motivational role in our maturation since we do not achieve optimal development amid environmental ease. Character and soul growth involve many aspects of rigorous problem solving. Not only are repeated decisions and hard work necessary for achievement, but the toughening educational episodes of frustration, disappointment, and failure are also indispensable contributors to the development of integrity and stamina.

The spiritually mature are not thwarted or discouraged by opposition to spiritual goals and objectives. Such problems challenge them to greater effort and inspire them to develop more effective strategies in the struggle. The Supreme triumphs in our lives and in the universe through never-ceasing evolutionary incrementation. Persistence, more persistence, and Supreme persistence is the pathway to material, personal, and spiritual achievement.

### *Summary Statement*

Spiritual psychology is rooted in personal reality relationships; there is no substitute for experience. Experience is the existential means and catalyst of all human achievement and the cosmic cocoon of soul actualization. We must ever distinguish reality living from philosophizing about life, action from theory, and doing from dreaming. Spiritual growth requires evolutionary persistence. Character is the product of rigorous struggle, painful conflict, unyielding determination, steadfast faith, and progressive action.

✳ ✳ ✳

## 6. Methods of Growth: Transformation and Adjustment

Growth and adaptation are the principles of planetary survival. Organisms develop or they deteriorate. Human beings improve their physical fitness into the young adult years and then slowly decline in physiological abilities. Our mental and spiritual development, while related to corporeal competence, do not share these material limitations. For everyone the future is open to spiritual growth and mortal transcendence. The psychological disciplines of this road are exacting. We are free to choose among facts, meanings, and values. In doing so, the human pilgrimage is sometimes sidetracked by evil, the ignorant and unknowing violation of universe law; blocked by sin, the discerning and intentional disobedience of the divine will; or terminated by iniquity, a complete identification with unreality, whereby the individual commits spiritual suicide.

Most people grow up with a limited awareness of the spiritual dimension of existence and a partial commitment to eternal values. With increasing experience we discover that our choices and our mental attitudes are basic to all aspects of human effectiveness. We learn to overcome obstacles and solve problems by using our minds. Through loyalty to appealing values and creative imagination we learn to transcend the limitations of our environment. The pain of experience teaches us the limits of sensual pleasure and the satisfactions of fair play and loving relationships. We become aware of the growing importance of an authentic leading deep within that is usually associated with a reality beyond ourselves—God. At some critical point in our lives the culminating effect of these value experiences leads us to a personal encounter with the Indwelling Presence of God.

When we commit our lives to our Heavenly Father, even though we may not be fully aware of it, a revolutionary event has taken place in our mind and soul. Our act of volitional dedication and spiritual allegiance is a cognitive transformational event, opening our lives to a new level of spiritual growth and power. No deprivation of opportunity or ability can stop this ascending adventure in the kingdom of God. In this will decision we have taken the critical step in the psychological reorganization or consolidation and consecration of all our values, incentives, and motivation. What knowledge, reason, and sheer will power could not do, faith, insight, and mind transformation accomplishes through spiritual power. It liberates us from being confined to physical level options and limits. In essence, we have been born again; it is a destiny direction of our own choosing. We have a new identity which fully recognizes and accepts our status as a son or daughter of God with all of the privileges and obligations that this birthright entails.

Now we must grow in this new or fully accepted selfhood into robust spiritual strength and beauty. How drastically this conversion or dedication experience changes our lives depends mainly on two things: where we were before this psychological transformation took place and the maturity we have achieved in volitional constancy and mind mastery. When the mind is prepared and ready, sudden changes are possible. Usually the consolidation of psychological resources, the marshaling of courageous will persistence, and spiritual growth are required before we can control, master, and redirect our animal impulses, drives, and emotions. Our aspirations and ideals spring forth in geometric proliferation but our ability to actualize them in living proceeds at an arithmetic pace. Consequently, our growth takes place mostly through evolutionary adjustment, which is now and then interspersed and assisted by spiritual transformation events.

We should welcome dissatisfaction with the current quality of our lives, but not become discouraged with the slow progress we make in changing it. As we hunger for growth, our faithful striving and supreme desires eventually determine what we will become. Because we are Spirit indwelt, the potentials of our personality are dominant over actuals; our moment-by-moment achievements fashion our destiny. It takes time, wisdom, and concentrated effort to reconcile our animal and spiritual natures. Inescapable conflict is encountered in going from the life of the flesh to the life of the Spirit, from egocentric orientation to reality centeredness.

Selfish and sensual urges are not suppressed by religious rules or legal prohibitions. Neither can they be banished by will power. Just as a steam boiler generates steam as long as there is a fire in the fire box, so our animal passions are fueled as long as they occupy our consciousness. Negative attention directed toward control or abstinence is almost as effective in generating desire as positive contemplation anticipating fulfillment. As long as there is conscious visualization in the psychological fire box of attention, the steam of desire is being generated. We must find ways to redirect the generating power of need consciousness. In the same way that two objects cannot reside in the same space at the same time, two thoughts cannot occupy the mind at the same moment. Substitutionary thought control is the pathway to determining motivational direction. It is a rigorous and repetitious discipline but the sure road to mind mastery.

Transcendence of our animal nature is achieved through the constant renewal of our mind until spiritual frames of reference become spontaneous and habitual. We need to faith-visualize, actually "live in" the new insight, attitude, emotion, or spiritually motivated action that we wish to become a part of our lives. This process of restructuring our mind and behavior is slow but unfailingly effective. We must expect to endure periods of the pain of hunger and the suffering of deprivation, but these trials are soon replaced by the joy of mastery and the vigor of physical, psychological, and spiritual fitness. The direction of the Spirit involves effort, conflict, struggle, suffering, persistence, and undaunted faith; but the rewards of spiritual-religious living are growth, character integrity, wholeness, competency, inner peace, joy, and the highest human happiness and fulfillment.

The changes of growth are associated with action, service, and time. Spiritual development is largely an unconscious process. Slight alterations in our thinking or feeling sometimes take place on the subliminal level of consciousness and occasionally a sudden transformation results from a new and stirring insight. Ordinarily, however, our reasoning and ideals are far in advance of our feeling and emotions. Spiritual maturity unifies our intellectual, volitional, and emotional natures. At some point in our pilgrimage our temperament or inner life achieves freedom from the coercions of physiological, social, and environmental cues. Our identity as sons or daughters of God transcends all other references and we are filled with the joy and radiance of those who live in spiritual frames of reference.

Spiritual growth is not a straight-line experience. Typically, we have relapses and setbacks which require rededication, readjustment, and renewed effort. Even when we have solidified levels of achievement, we are not permitted to enjoy our accomplishments for very long. Soon new insights, new transformations, and new adjustments demand our attention and effort. This is a constant life process as long as we are willing to grow.

As personality development matures, achievement is more rapid and less traumatic. In individuals who have achieved good mind control, psychological spiritual transformation can quickly readjust attitudes, emotions, and behaviors. These changes become less drastic and are assimilated as a natural response to expanded reality insight. We are learning how to convert the difficulties of time into the steppingstones of spiritual achievement. Such spiritual living transforms mediocre individuals into people of power.

### *Summary Statement*

The critical turning point of spiritual psychology is the moment in which we commit our lives to the Heavenly Father. This cognitive transformation event opens us to a new level of spiritual growth and power. The actualization of our new status is orchestrated by a dialectic between sudden spiritual transformation and personal evolutionary adjustment, culminating in spiritual growth. Through mind mastery the Indwelling Spirit unifies our inner life, frees us from physiological, egocentric, and social coercions, and fills us with the joy of those who live in spiritual frames of reference. The Universal Father uses this psychological process to transform mediocre individuals into people of power.

* * *

## 7. Basic Actions: Loving Fellowship, Creative Work, and Fulfilling Service

When we truly believe something, we act upon it. Anyone who has had a vital experience with truth, beauty, or goodness must share it with others. Living faith invariably creates a highly active personality. We can be reserved and objective about our social theories and religious philosophy, but we become missionary evangels of those spiritual values which have transformed our lives. An individual who is dedicated to spiritual ideals lives and works to actualize this inner guidance. A religious person transforms faith into practice. Such activity inclinations are indigenous to the divine plan for human development. Gaining an understanding of God the Supreme requires growth and accomplishment in our lives. The primary channels through which this personality evolvement takes place are in our relationships with other people and in the activities that provide the necessities of living.

The basic action inspired by spiritual experience is love and fellowship. We are social beings who need the identity, support, stimulation, and love of other people. Although we, as children of God, recognize all people as our spiritual brothers and sisters, our finitude limits the actualization of this universal relationship. We are only capable of engaging in practical, working relationships with a relatively small number of people. The family is not only the most important human institution, but it is the ideal model for all social relationships. In group interactions where spiritual values are dominant there is an atmosphere of love and communion. A practical measure of the spiritual quality of our minds is the extent of our love for the people with whom we associate.

The most important activities of our lives are family and friendship relationships. Human nature needs the stimulus and fellowship of social interaction to develop spiritual character. Real joy and happiness cannot be experienced in isolation. We learn most from family and small group relationships. Just as family members do not think alike or behave in the same way, so members of larger social institutions should learn how to debate and disagree and yet be sympathetic with other views and supportive of people with different lifestyles. Unity of purpose can be experienced in the midst of the diversity of ways in which we actualize our collective ideals. People working together in harmony toward social objectives are far more effective than the mere sum of their efforts. United action results in a geometric culmination of achievement for the common good. Historically, the most innovative discoveries and contributions to society have been made by small groups. Small cohesive groups of people united in common projects make up the growing edge of culture and civilization.

The culminating aspect of all family and group activities is service. It is the spiritual objective of human life. The sincere desire to contribute to the welfare of individuals and society should be the God-like aspiration of all human beings. It is the spiritual quality that binds and builds marriage, family life, and social institutions. Such service produces the fruits of the spirit independent of reward or opposition. We achieve loving, supporting, and healing ways of living which undergird individuals, strengthen social institutions, and make our world a better place in which to live.

In addition to the fellowship and service which we give to our fellow human beings, the major contribution which we make to life and the kingdom of God is in our working career. Whether in the home, field, or larger society, we spend most of our lives serving in some fashion in the social economy. If we are fortunate, this work is creative activity which is satisfying as well as financially rewarding. Unless we have found such pleasant and purposeful work for our lives, it becomes aimless and unfulfilling. We discover such a formative design for our holistic development which stimulates the flowering of our abilities by looking deep within.

The Indwelling Spirit of God has an ideal plan for our lives. This plan is not related primarily to a specific vocation but to our moral, mental, and spiritual enrichment and progress. It is concerned with our total personality development. Each person has a natural configuration of abilities and inclinations toward certain types of activity and achievement. Our optimum growth and maturation depends on our discerning and following this divine plan, which utilizes these natural abilities.

As we meditate on inner creative leadings, we acquire a sense of God's will for our lives from which we may formulate goals and purposes. The real character and substance of our personal development begins when we actualize these spiritual urges into specific projects of living which eventually take the form of a life plan. This plan, this sense of calling and partnership with God, gives meaning and direction to life, and with it, a new source of energy and strength. There is a sense that we are in the right place, serving where we belong. As we grow spiritually, we are increasingly able to solve personal, social, and economic problems. We are learning to utilize the energy of spiritual power to operate the mechanisms of material and intellectual achievement.

The avenues of service are as broad as the needs and interests of humanity. The uniqueness of service is the result of human creativity. Although every culture shares common knowledge and values, the individual experiences a different combination of facts, meanings, and values; as these factors are assimilated in the process of living, each person achieves a new and creative expression of universe values. The quality of our creativity is proportional to our abilities and spiritual attunement. Creative activity is our ultimate intrinsic response to God's presence in our lives; it is superb play resulting in reality enhancement. We are most creative when we lose ourselves in a larger cause and a greater reality. Human creativity augments the soul, enlarges our personality awareness, and contributes to the world.

Although creative service is an intrinsic activity which we enjoy as an end in itself, all vocational and avocational tasks have aspects of work we do not like but which must be done. These monotonous or onerous routines can become meaningful and semi-enjoyable when associated with the underlying purpose of our lives. No work should be regarded as "common labor" as all extrinsic activity can be dignified as a service to our fellows and God through its linkage with the central goals of our mortal career.

Facilitating service is one of the chief objectives of spiritual psychology. It is a dedication of our lives to helping others; contributing to truth, beauty, and goodness on our planet; the creation of that which will make the world a better place in which to live. Humanistic workers can produce social results of value, but spiritual servers generate spiritual fruit which transforms individuals and society. Secular sociologists make studies of human problems and leave people largely unchanged. For spiritual workers, knowledge is only a means to an end; they concentrate on changing people, correcting error and injustice, and turning society around. Service is both the channel through which we are actualizing the will of God in our lives and the greatest source of human happiness and fulfillment.

Following the guidance of the spirit is never easy. Spirit-indited tasks push us to our limits. The direction of the Spirit requires hard work, struggle, conflict, determination, persistent effort, and indomitable faith. Spiritual pioneers always meet with disapproval and opposition. As we react positively, wisely, and aggressively in meeting the frustrations and harassments of progressive living, we become more resourceful in our service. Kingdom builders take inescapable hardships in stride; difficulties invigorate their efforts and obstacles inspire them to greater resolve.

Our responsibility is to act; the results are in larger hands. Loyalty to spiritual vision causes us to enthusiastically plant saplings whose mature shade we will never enjoy. Second-milers do not expect rewards or immediate results. They live in the Supreme's evolutionary frame of reference and faith-visualize the fruition of their labors. Having the courage to be and to act, they are, nonetheless, rewarded by unexpected discoveries and unforeseen accomplishments. They abide in the confident assurance that eternal truth, transcendent beauty, unceasing good will, and boundless love will conquer the world!

### *Summary Statement*

Facilitating service is one of the chief objectives of spiritual psychology. True religion demands that we *do* something. Our Indwelling Spirit has an ideal plan for our lives. The primary requirements of this plan are loving fellowship and creative action, both of which achieve their highest expression in service. Following the guidance of the spirit is never easy; it pushes us to our limits. Our responsibility is to act; the results are worked out in the divine overcontrol of creative evolution. Eternal truth, transcendent beauty, unceasing goodwill, and boundless love will conquer the world!

* * *

## C.

## THE THREE DEFINITIVE CHARACTERISTICS OF SPIRITUAL LIVING
## (The Results)

### 1. Inner Peace

Inner peace is the underlying attitude of those who have found their identity as sons or daughters of God. We have committed ourselves to follow the Father's will and are striving to actualize his plan for our lives; therefore, we are confident and sure about the ultimates of our destiny. A sense of spiritual security undergirds our lives which nothing can remove.

Material things are seen as temporary conveniences which do not govern our lives and whose loss does not threaten our inner stability. Devotion to spiritual realities has liberated us from the demands of ego importance and the need for social approval. Even though our outer lives may be surrounded by chaos and danger, our inner self is calm and secure. It is, indeed, a peace which passes all understanding. Such spiritual stability is immune to disappointment.

## 2. Integration, Balance, and Wholeness

The psychology of spiritual living is characterized by integration, balance, and wholeness. The centrality of God in our lives structures all of our values and priorities. Everything in our personality makeup finds its place in integrated effectiveness because all of our knowledge and abilities are ordered and arranged by our dedication to Ultimate Reality. Spiritual goals and purposes unify our talents and resources. We are traveling wholeheartedly in one direction, free from crippling conflicts and cross purposes. As energy systems, psychological systems, and spiritual systems are integrated in experience, a strong and creative personality develops.

Spiritual living is living in harmony with reality. Physical, mental, and spiritual aspects of experience are balanced, integrated, and harmonized. Religious living produces a well-balanced personality and an integrity of character not explained by the laws of physiology, psychology, and sociology. Stability and balance in character are always proportional to spiritual attainment.

Human nature has a deep longing for fulfillment and wholeness. As our soul evolves and our personality develops, there is an effective integration of material, mindal, and spiritual resources. We become more balanced and wise in our comprehension of truth, representation of beauty, and actualization of goodness. Through the synergistic dynamics of spiritual power we are made more whole, effective, and real.

### 3. Joy and Happiness

The God-saturated soul is filled with irrepressible joy and happiness. Zest for living is born of the inner realization that we are undergirded and nourished by the inexhaustible power and loving personalities of a limitless universe, created and controlled by our Universal Father. When we are sure about God and willing to be led by his Indwelling Spirit, we are joyful and happy; we live in the reality awareness of being his sons and daughters.

Happiness has its inception in our psychological-spiritual identity and orientation, not in our environmental surroundings. It is closely related to, and partially the product of, unconditional love. Motivated by the urge for creative service, we lose ourselves in spirit-directed achievement and one day discover our lives are overflowing with happiness. Finding enhanced techniques of emotional satisfaction through the pursuit of worthy goals fills us with a superb sense of well-being. The highest happiness is inseparably linked with spiritual progress.

#### *Summary Statement*

Those who have found their identity as children of God, who are sure about ultimates, have a sense of security and inner peace which is indestructible. The psychology of spiritual living is characterized by integration, balance, and wholeness. The God-saturated soul is filled with irrepressible joy and zest for living. The highest happiness is inseparably linked with spiritual progress.

✻ ✻ ✻

## D.

## THE THREE CULMINATING OBJECTIVES OF SPIRITUAL LIVING
**(The Rewards)**

### 1. God Consciousness

The most important objective in human life is to establish communication and fellowship with the Indwelling Spirit of God. The electrochemical energy circuits of the brain are so dominant that it is difficult for our minds to make contact with the supermaterial and superideational communications of the Indwelling Spirit. As we develop and discipline our minds to the sensitivity of truth, beauty, and goodness, we become aware of a spiritual dimension of reality. We intuit the presence of a quiet, loving guidance. This subliminal communion with God becomes the most real experience of our lives. We strive to more faithfully follow the leading of this divine monitor and to more cheerfully pursue the tasks assigned to us. God consciousness is synonymous with integrating ourselves with the highest spiritual reality in the universe. It is our assurance of an eternal destiny.

### 2. Oneness with God: Salvation

Mortals evolve a spiritual nature by progressive reciprocal communion with God and intelligent conformity to the divine will. Through gradual attunement with the Indwelling Spirit of God, at some point in our universe career we become one with this Fragment of the Universal Father. While none of our personality and identity is ever lost or diffused, this fusion gives us a more brilliant focus, a greater spiritual enhancement, and makes us more real. A new order of being emerges for unending universe service. This is salvation from material restrictions, incompleteness of self, time, and finite limits of growth. No limit can be placed on the potential destiny of this new divine-human creation.

### 3. Eternal Service Destiny

We live in a gigantic cosmos populated by countless material beings and celestial personalities. There is an eternal purpose of ever-ascending significance for each individual who chooses to do the will of the Universal Father. Our universe education and spiritual growth begins in earnest when our mortal sojourn ends and we are resurrected on more advanced worlds for progressive experience and service. We have begun an endless unfolding of eternal educational experience dominated by challenging adventure, thrilling service, and spiritual attainment. Human imagination is too limited to grasp its future possibilities. Yet we lowly human beings even now can enjoy the opportunities of this ever-widening career in mastering the principles of spiritual psychology.

* * *

## E.
## PRINCIPLES OF MINISTRY

If you have experienced a dynamic personal relationship with God and have dedicated yourself to the opportunities of this divine-human interaction, you are motivated to serve in the actualization of spiritual values in the world. Service is the natural and authentic personality expression of sons and daughters of God.

There are innumerable ways in which you can minister to people and society. By searching within, you will discover the activities which you find most creative and rewarding, or the task to which you feel called. God can be served through any vocation or constructive human activity. Since everyone is unique, each person develops a special kind and quality of contribution to society; therefore, the Universal Father's symphony of service is rich in its variety of benefits and ministrations to humanity.

Whatever the occupation, service, or activity in which you are engaged, the quality and effectiveness of that service depends largely on how it is carried out. Over and above the technical qualifications basic to your service, the amount of good which you are able to contribute to humankind is significantly augmented by following the seven spiritual principles of ministry.

### 1. Use Wisdom

Use wisdom and balance in all of your service. Avoid extremes, exhibitionism, oversell, and the spectacular. Learn to distinguish between artistic good taste and the theatrical. Remember that personal contact is more effective than impersonal mass communication. Understand the wisdom and effectiveness of small groups. These groups form coalitions and networks more open and dynamic than hierarchical bureaucracies and self-serving cults. Such a network is many times greater than the sum of its parts. It has multiple leadership, pluralistic policies, and its center is everywhere. Start where people are, not where you are. Communicate in their frames of reference and anticipate their natural reactions. Combine the most expert knowledge with the highest values in all of your ministry. Master your mind through the power of the Spirit. Be strong in the Spirit; know that in liaison with God nothing can defeat the spiritual purposes of your life. Be fearless but act with discretion.

### 2. Let Love Create

Let love create the atmosphere of all of your interpersonal relationships. Remember that you cannot communicate effectively with others unless you positively and unconditionally accept them with all of their imperfections. Strive to prevent your own biases and limitations from interfering or distorting your service to them. Support, stimulate, and help people; do not seek to coerce them. See all of your fellows as persons of worth and strive to build their self-confidence and self-respect. Be natural and genuine and enjoy their company. Serve out of love, a thankful heart, and the joy of the act itself. Ministry is an intrinsic activity of the creative mind and the loving soul. Extrinsic motivation in service compromises its spiritual value. Serving God even for good extrinsic purposes, such as building your religious organization or even to bring about a spiritual renaissance, limits its spiritual value and personal satisfaction. Minister out of the intrinsic motivation of love, thankfulness, and joy; and the extrinsic repercussions or results will largely take care of themselves. Serve in the openness of creative love but do not try to manipulate people.

### 3. Cultivate Openness

Temper your personal convictions with philosophical objectivity. Always be honest and open. Cultivate freedom of opinion and respect the right of others to disagree with your most deeply held convictions. Honor each person's God-given right to self-determination. Try to establish common ground but do not contend with people. Let your enthusiasm for truth animate your discussions but never knowingly put people down or offend.

### 4. Cooperate With Evolution

Recognize that evolution is the underlying principle of life. Do not expect immediate results. All growth is subliminal, beyond our direct conscious control, and has mustard-seed beginnings. The roots of a new tree of life take decades to penetrate the rocks of tradition on which it is planted. Be patient but do not become the victim of a fearful "do-nothing" psychology and bury your talents and treasure in the bogs of stagnation or the quagmires of cult obscurities. Be concerned about ministering effectively but relatively unconcerned about results. Realize that your ministry must be planned and conducted in the context of the law of readiness. Always minister at the point of evolutionary readiness but do not confuse this basic preparation for the surface conditions of psychological and social readiness. All who have prophetic vision know that evolution, the plow of history, eventually breaks the crust of individual resistance and moves the clods of social stagnation. Be loyal and persistent in your service without needing to see results or to be honored by success. It is our privilege and responsibility to minister; the results are in the hands of God the Supreme. In all things, cultivate in yourself the mind and attitude of the Supreme. The vicissitudes of time do not change the goals of eternity.

### 5. Live With the Commonplace

Be actively involved in routine, commonplace experiences. Grow, bloom, and bear fruit in the soil where you are planted. If possible, keep your old social and religious ties strong and healthy. Share at the level of spiritual acceptance. When you are a caterpillar do not live under the illusion that you are a butterfly or an eagle. Only dedicated and creative "caterpillaring" will bring you inner satisfaction and a sense of fulfillment. These mundane activities and identifications will bring a sense of proportion, genuineness, and integrity to your ministry. Forget the failures of the past and do not allow yourself to be preoccupied anticipating the future. Live in the present in constant fellowship with the Father and absorbed in the existential moment of experience.

### 6. Develop a Sense of Humor

Cultivate an active sense of humor. Humor helps us maintain a proper sense of perspective. You can carry man- or woman-sized loads when you get the world off your shoulders. Do not take yourself too seriously even though you are participating in important work. Be unconcerned about prestige and status. Strive to avoid self-contemplation and cultivate self-forgetfulness. Finite personalities can become tragic figures when they lose their sense of perspective and fail to appreciate the comedy of life. We need to laugh at ourselves and the frustrating, ridiculous, and absurd situations we encounter. A light-hearted spirit can be a great asset in carrying the sometimes heavy burdens of ministry.

### 7. Serve With Joy

Above all, live with joy in your heart and find joy in your service. You belong to the Father's kingdom which has an eternal future of unimaginable adventure and reward. Nothing can long prevent the fulfillment of your most ardent spiritual hopes and fondest dreams. All who experience this faith in an eternal destiny live with irrepressible joy even in the midst of material hardship, social conflict, and seeming personal defeat. As you free yourself from the slavery of the lure of things, the adoration or criticism of people, and the importance or preoccupation with self, you will experience the liberating joys of service. You will also discover that in doing so you are free from the egocentric social pressure to be successful or to maintain a reputation. When your will is in harmony with the will of God, the life of service also brings a deep inner peace. The meaningfulness and joy of worship and service transcend the rewards of all other human activities.

## CONCLUDING STATEMENT

Spiritual psychology seeks to clarify and augment those mental processes which help us to know God and follow his will in our lives. Spiritual living culminates in refreshing worship and loving service. In this brief review of the realities, determiners, characteristics, and objectives of spiritual living, we have summarized the basic and universal psychological principles germane to the divine-human dialogue. Many aspects of the nature of reality are not mentioned or discussed in these pages. This is only a primer.

If you are interested, I would urge you to study more complete presentations of spiritual enlightenment and expanded insight. Kenneth Boulding in *The Meaning of the Twentieth Century*, Alvin Toffler in *The Third Wave*, John Naisbitt in *Megatrends*, Fritjof Capra in *The Turning Point*, and many other prophetic voices have pointed out that we are entering a major transitional change in the history of humanity. Viktor Frankl, in *Man's Search for Meaning* and *Man's Search for Ultimate Meaning*, and Roberto Assagioli in *Psychosynthesis* give further support for understanding the spiritual-psychological aspect of humankind. We desperately need spiritual foundations which are large enough, solid enough, and have the visionary potential to give stability and guidance to the new age which is struggling to be born.

There are many pathways to spiritual Reality. The Spirit of God is active among all cultures, religions, and peoples. Prophets are speaking at the growing edge of all segments of our human society. If you become an honest and dedicated seeker for truth without placing limitations on its origin, the Father's Indwelling Spirit will lead you to those sources and experiences which will inspire your spiritual growth and enlightenment beyond your present imagination. It is eternally true that "those who seek will find." And when we become seekers, we discover with Habakkuk, "Look… there is work being done in your day which will astonish you and you would not believe if you were told." (1:5)

You must discover this new and enlarged spiritual truth for yourself. No second-hand knowledge is spiritually authentic. To be convincing and real, it must be personally perceived and experienced. May our Universal Father's Spirit inspire and guide you in your search to enrich and enlarge the limited spiritual insights of this primer.

* * *

# INDEX

Meredith Justin Sprunger is a minister in the United Church of Christ and a college professor, now retired from pastoral and teaching responsibilities. He has served congregations in the midwest and taught at Elmhurst College and the Indiana Institute of Technology, functioning as the head of the Department of Psychology, Chair of the Division of Liberal Arts, and President.

For many years he was involved as a counselor and psychological consultant, holding a Private Practice Certificate in Psychology in the state of Indiana. He served as editor of *The Spiritual Fellowship Journal*, an ecumenical publication.

www.ingramcontent.com/pod-product-compliance
Lightning Source LLC
LaVergne TN
LVHW091006080826
845145LV00003B/1142

* 9 7 8 0 9 8 2 4 2 7 8 8 0 *